AFRICAN WORLD HISTORIES

Colonial Africa,
1884–1994

AFRICAN WORLD HISTORIES

Series Editor
Trevor R. Getz, San Francisco State University

African World Histories is a series of retellings of some of the most commonly discussed episodes of the African and global past from the perspectives of Africans who lived through them. Accessible yet scholarly, African World Histories gives students insights into African experiences concerning many of the events and trends that are commonly discussed in the history classroom.

Titles in the Series

Published
Cosmopolitan Africa, 1700–1875
Trevor R. Getz, San Francisco State University

Colonial Africa, 1884–1994
Dennis Laumann, University of Memphis

Forthcoming
Slavery and the Atlantic Slave Trade, 1400–1800
Kwasi Konadu, City University of New York
Trevor Getz, San Francisco State University

Sovereignty and Struggle, 1945–1994
Jonathan T. Reynolds, Northern Kentucky University
Christopher Saunders, University of Cape Town

Africanizing Democracies, 1980–Present
Alicia Decker, Purdue University
Andrea Arrington, University of Arkansas

AFRICAN WORLD HISTORIES

Colonial Africa

1884–1994

Dennis Laumann

University of Memphis

New York   Oxford
OXFORD UNIVERSITY PRESS

In memory of DeMadre Kareem Lockett

Oxford University Press is a department of the University of Oxford. It furthers the
University's objective of excellence in research, scholarship, and education by
publishing worldwide.

Oxford   New York
Auckland   Cape Town   Dar es Salaam   Hong Kong   Karachi
Kuala Lumpur   Madrid   Melbourne   Mexico City   Nairobi
New Delhi   Shanghai   Taipei   Toronto

With offices in
Argentina   Austria   Brazil   Chile   Czech Republic   France   Greece
Guatemala   Hungary   Italy   Japan   Poland   Portugal   Singapore
South Korea   Switzerland   Thailand   Turkey   Ukraine   Vietnam

For titles covered by Section 112 of the US Higher Education
Opportunity Act, please visit www.oup.com/us/he for the latest
information about pricing and alternate formats.

Published by Oxford University Press.
198 Madison Avenue, New York, New York 10016
http://www.oup.com

Library of Congress Cataloging-in-Publication Data

Laumann, Dennis, 1970–
African world histories: colonial Africa, 1884–1994 / Dennis Laumann.
    p. cm.
Includes index.
ISBN 978-0-19-979639-7
1. Africa—Colonization.   2. Africa—History—1884–1960.   3. Africa—History—1960–
I. Title.
DT29.L38 2012
960.3—dc23
2012017010

About the Cover: *Colonie belge 2*, a painting by Tshibumba Kanda Matulu of present-day
Democratic Republic of Congo, circa 1971. Tshibumba's work chronicles the tragic history of colo-
nial and postcolonial Congo, such as this depiction of forced laborers being supervised by Force
Publique soliders brandishing the dreaded *chicotte*.

9 8 7 6
Printed in the United States of America
on acid-free paper

CONTENTS

Maps And Figures

Maps

Figures

Preface

This book is meant to provide a general overview of the European colonial occupation of Africa. Although what is regarded as the colonial period in African history was relatively recent and brief, a survey presents significant challenges. First, the generally recognized time span of colonial Africa, roughly 1884 to 1960, is not accurate for many parts of the continent. European settlement in southern Africa began in the seventeenth century, for example, and white minority rule did not end there until 1994. Second, the subject of African colonial history has generated a wealth of literature, especially of late, so giving readers a sense of all the various trends and developments requires a great deal of sifting. Third, and last, some specialists in particular countries, areas, or topics may rightly feel that their subject has not received adequate attention, but in a concise volume such as this one, which covers more than a century of history spanning an entire continent, it is impossible to analyze every aspect of colonial Africa. I therefore have attempted to address the major themes in this history, in a chronological fashion, by highlighting major and informative case studies throughout this book. A short list of references comprising some of the works cited as well as additional relevant, noteworthy texts is included at the end of each chapter. While my own opinions and findings make their way into the narrative, the purpose of this book is to present a balanced, readable, and comprehensive overview of how Africans experienced European colonial rule.

A number of people and institutions deserve recognition for the support they provided during the process of researching and writing this book. First and foremost, I thank series editor Trevor R. Getz for asking me to write it and generously guiding me with his advice. Likewise, thanks to Charles Cavaliere, our editor at Oxford University Press, for his enthusiasm and understanding throughout this project. It has been a pleasure working with our diligent and gracious assistant editor at Oxford, Lauren Aylward.

To help me complete this book, the University of Memphis awarded me a sabbatical in spring 2011, and my chair, Janann Sherman, offered research and travel support. While in Memphis,

I spent much of my sabbatical working at Rhodes College, thanks to my good friend Mark Behr. The African Studies Center at the University of Florida hosted me as a visiting research scholar in February 2011. I benefited enormously from its lively program of lectures as well as many informal get-togethers, especially conversations with historians Sean Hanretta, Susan O'Brien, and Luise White. I thank then-director Leonardo A. Villalón for extending an invitation to Gainesville and associate director Todd H. Leedy for arranging my visit. I also thank the people who reviewed the manuscript:

Esperanza Brizuela-Garcia, Montclair State University	Carina Ray, Fordham University
Maxim Matusevich, Seton Hall University	William K. Storey, Millsaps College
Michelle Moyd, Indiana University	Benjamin Talton, Temple University

My formal education as a historian of Africa began under the guidance of two remarkable teachers at Binghamton University, Ali A. Mazrui and Akbar Muhammad. That training continued in graduate school at UCLA, where Christopher Ehret, the late Boniface Obichere, and above all my advisor, Merrick Posnansky, imparted inspiration, knowledge, and precision, all of which I hope is manifested in this book.

As always, I am indebted to my family—especially my wife Rebecca, my son Max, my father Heinz, and my brother Thomas—for their love and support. I regret my late mother Renate could not hold these pages in her hands.

This book is dedicated in memory of a beloved student who left this world way too early but continually reminds me of why I teach African history.

About the Author

Dennis Laumann is associate professor of history at the University of Memphis. The author of the forthcoming *Remembering the Germans in Ghana* (Peter Lang) and other publications on West African history, Laumann received his doctorate from UCLA in 1999. He is president of the Ghana Studies Association and a Fulbright Scholar. He also is the recipient of numerous teaching honors, including the Thomas W. Briggs Foundation's Excellence in Teaching Award.

Series Introduction

The African World Histories series presents a new approach to teaching and learning for African history and African studies courses. Its main innovation is to interpret African and global experiences from the perspectives of the Africans who lived through them. By integrating accounts and representations produced or informed by Africans with accessible scholarly analysis at both local and global levels, African World Histories gives students insight into Africans' understandings and experiences of such episodes as the Atlantic slave trade, the growth of intercontinental commerce and the industrial revolution, colonialism, and the Cold War. The authors in this series look at these episodes through the lenses of culture, politics, social organization, daily life, and economics in an integrated format informed by recent scholarly studies as well as primary source materials. Unlike those of many textbooks and series, the authors of African World Histories actively take positions on major questions, such as the centrality of violence in the colonial experience, the cosmopolitan nature of precolonial African societies, and the importance of democratization in Africa today. Underlying this approach is the belief that students can succeed when presented with relatively brief, jargon-free interpretations of African societies that integrate Africans' perspectives with critical interpretations and that balance intellectual rigor with broad accessibility.

This series is designed for use in both the world history and the African history/studies classroom. As an African history/studies teaching tool it combines continentwide narratives with emphases on specific, localized, and thematic stories that help demonstrate wider trends. As auxiliary texts for the world history classroom, the volumes in this series can help to illuminate important episodes in the global past from the perspectives of Africans, adding complexity and depth, as well as facilitating intellectual growth for students. Thus it will help world history students not only understand that the human past was "transnational" and shared, but also see how it was understood differently by different groups and individuals.

African World Histories is the product of a grand collaboration. The authors include scholars from around the world and across Africa. Each volume is reviewed by multiple professionals in African history and related fields. The excellent team of editors at Oxford University Press, led by Charles Cavaliere, put a great deal of effort into commissioning, reviewing, and bringing these volumes to publication. Finally, we all stand on the shoulders of early giants in the field, including Cheikh Anta Diop, Joseph Ki-Zerbo, Jan Vansina, and Roland Oliver.

— TREVOR R. GETZ, SERIES EDITOR

Introduction

What is colonialism? The word is often used without an understanding of its precise definition. We speak of the colonial world or the colonial experience or colonized minds, but what exactly do we mean? Colonialism generally refers to the seizure and occupation of territory (colonization) belonging to one group of people (the colonized) by another group of people (the colonizers). Sometimes colonization results in the actual settlement of the territory by the colonizers, but more often (especially in the case of European colonial rule in Africa) it only leads to the exploitation of the colony through minimal alien administration. The words *colonialism* and *imperialism* also tend to be used interchangeably and so have become confused. While imperialism is the essential basis for colonialism, the latter does not always follow the former. Imperialism is the process of one group of people extending its economic, political, or social power over other peoples. A nation can be imperialist by waging wars with neighboring and faraway states or undermining and dominating the economies of weaker nations without necessarily colonizing them. Yet, colonialism frequently is an extension of imperialism, as certainly occurred when European imperialists colonized Africa.

This book covers the history of the colonial era in African history, during which the entire continent (with the exceptions of Liberia and Ethiopia, which enjoyed varying degrees of independence throughout the period) was seized and occupied by Europeans. The colonization process gradually began in the mid–nineteenth century, a period of what scholars call informal colonialism but that accelerated and expanded dramatically in the 1880s. The Berlin Conference of 1884–1885, during which the European powers plotted their division of Africa among themselves, is normally considered the start of the colonial period. Within a decade or two, what European imperialists called the pacification of Africa was relatively speaking complete, though some areas of the continent were not fully colonized until the beginning of the twentieth century and resistance to colonial rule everywhere never ceased. The actual experience of colonialism in many parts of Africa was short-lived, however, as popular anticolonial movements exploded after the Second World War. By 1960, most Africans had regained their independence, as European colonists departed and new African nations were declared. Other Africans, particularly in southern Africa and in the Portuguese colonies, had to resort to armed struggle to win their independence, which came only in the last decades of the twentieth century. Our survey ends in 1994, when the apartheid regime in South Africa was replaced by a democratic, nonracial government headed by the first African president, Nelson Mandela. Thus, the colonial period lasted not even one century in most of Africa and far less in many parts of continent, although, as will be shown, far longer in both South Africa and Algeria.

It is often forgotten that the colonization of Africa by Europeans happened relatively recently in history. In fact, generally speaking, Africa was the last continent to come under European colonial rule. Most of the Americas were conquered by European powers, first by Spain and Portugal in the early sixteenth century, while by the late eighteenth century, Australia was effectively occupied by the British. And though many parts of Asia remained independent of European rule, large areas of the continent, including much of present-day India and parts of China, were colonized by Europeans as early as the eighteenth century. While it is true there were several small European colonies along Africa's coastlines—such as France's settlements in North Africa and West Africa, Portugal's enclaves in Central Africa, and Britain's Cape Town in the south—what we refer to as the colonial period in African history, again, did not start until the late nineteenth century. Until then, Europeans did not possess sufficient technological advantages, including military, to take over Africa; neither did they have the desire or need to, since economic relations between European and African powers were, for the most part in the centuries before colonialism, mutually beneficial.

So, what changed in the nineteenth century? For the first time in history, Europeans surpassed Africa in technological superiority. Inventions such as the steamship and the railway, products of the industrial revolution spurred by the development of capitalism, allowed Europeans to extend their reach into the interior of Africa. Previously, European traders were not only restricted to their coastal forts and bases by the edicts of African rulers, but they simply did not have the means to sail up river or traverse vast land distances. Once they established themselves in the interior, the telegraph, another invention of the time, allowed efficient and secure communication between far-flung stations. In the 1850s, the discovery that quinine, a medicine derived from the bark of a tree, helped prevent and treat malaria (so much the scourge of Europeans in West Africa that it was known as the "white man's graveyard") and led to a gradual growth in the numbers of European traders, missionaries, and so-called explorers in Africa. Finally, Europeans created a powerful, brutally effective new weapon, the machine gun, which gave them an enormous military advantage over African armies in their own territories. As will be shown in chapter 1, it was not just that this new technology made colonization possible, but by the mid–nineteenth century, Europeans imperial powers actually had the desire and need to colonize Africa for economic and political reasons.

STUDY OF THE COLONIAL PERIOD

In light of these facts, that the colonization of Africa occurred quite recently in world history and lasted only several decades in many parts of the continent, we must assess the colonial period's importance in Africa's history. Several questions, each generated by different interpretations of the colonial period, can guide our assessment. For example, was the colonial era just a brief, even insignificant "episode," as the Nigerian historian Jacob Ade Ajayi proclaimed, considering that the long history of the African continent stretches back from human origins to the present? After all, why should we place so much emphasis on several decades, the 1880s to 1960s in most parts of Africa, in a history covering thousands and thousands of years? And, then, does it make sense to divide up this immense period into precolonial, colonial, and postcolonial periods when almost all of African history occurred in the first category (and which we further could split up innumerable ways, such as ancient, classical, medieval, etc.)? Historians who embrace a more Afrocentric perspective tend to argue this point.

Or was colonialism such a transformative era, one that so dramatically and irreversibly changed Africa's economic, social, and political institutions that it should continue to be afforded a special status in African history? In other words, is Africa after colonial rule so different from what it was before the colonial era that the aforementioned pre- and post- eras should remain blanketed around the colonial period? This is the more conventional understanding of the colonial period, one reflected in most scholarship.

Or is there a third possibility, lately proposed by historians of Africa, that colonialism was more of a continuum in African history? Yes, they argue, colonial rule undoubtedly was the imposition of foreign political rule and economic domination, but its impact was uneven across the continent and it did not fully prevent the continued development of African institutions within and beyond the colonial state. Furthermore, they propose, Africans were instrumental in the colonial process, too, not simply the bystanders or victims of colonial rule, but active shapers of colonialism, people who frequently viewed colonialism as an opportunity.

That last point is especially revealing as it marks a departure from traditional scholarship on colonialism, which tended to divide Africans into "collaborators" and "resisters." In this view, Africans either benefited from colonial rule at the expense of their fellow Africans or they fought against European domination through various peaceful and violent means. Today, scholars realize that the moral choices individuals faced usually were not that clear-cut and that it is simplistic to label Africans in one category or the other. For instance, should we consider a Lunda man who entered the Belgian colonial service in order to improve his status and provide for his family but who also, in the evenings, attended services at an African church where Europeans were depicted as vampires and anti-colonial sentiments were expressed a selfish collaborator? Or, on the other hand, was the Mande soldier who fought against French colonization in West Africa as part of an army that also captured and enslaved other Africans a heroic resister? This does not mean that there were no obvious cases of collaboration or resistance, but the reality of colonialism was far more complex to warrant the attachment to such acute, rigid dichotomies.

These perspectives on the colonial period are reflected in the origins, development, and current state of the historical literature on the subject. The creation of African history as an academic field outside of Africa coincided with the widespread end of colonial rule on the continent and the prevailing global anti-colonial sentiment following the Second World War. Whereas during the colonial era imperial powers were motivated to learn about the people they colonized in order to more effectively control them, some have argued that when the independence era began (and perhaps continuing until today) Africanists (specialists on Africa) played a similar role in helping to "make sense" of Africa to a Western audience. In the 1960s, the first courses in African history were taught in Europe and the United States, not in Africa where the legacy of colonial, Eurocentric education was entrenched and where there were few established universities. Nevertheless, a group of African historians, men who studied in Europe during the colonial era, began producing books on Africa's past. At first their work largely bypassed the colonial era—perhaps it was considered too recent and maybe even humiliating to examine—as historians focused on the precolonial era, especially the trade and politics of African states. In part, this coincided with the effort to highlight the glories of Africa's past, not only as an anecdote to the racist, colonial-era notion that Africa had no history before European rule but also as a precedent for the newly founded African nations. If the colonial era was simply a short episode of foreign domination, it was argued, Africa's leaders should look to the precolonial era for authentic, indigenous examples of leadership and administration.

Later in the 1960s, historians began studying colonialism more extensively, and two distinct approaches emerged. The first approach, carried out mainly by conservative, Western scholars, analyzed colonial administration and stressed what they believed to be the positive aspects of colonialism. In other words, the studies they produced examined the policies and procedures of European colonial officials and the infrastructure they built and the services they provided. In many ways, this literature carried on the "imperial history" of the colonial era, which focused on the lives of Europeans in Africa but barely mentioned Africans. The second approach, pursued by radical scholars, many based in Africa, concentrated on African resistance to colonialism. To counter the pro-imperialist literature and in their effort to show African agency during the colonial era, they wrote about the various ways Africans opposed European rule and fought for their independence. These historians distinguished between what was termed "active" and "passive" resistance as well as the localized armed uprisings of the early colonial period and the mass-based, nationalist, anti-colonial movements of late colonialism. This body of work was very influential in our understanding of the colonial period and in many respects formed the foundation of subsequent scholarly research.

The late 1960s also witnessed the growth of scholarship influenced by Marxism, which sharply criticized and rejected any positive portrayal of colonialism. In general, Marxist historians focus on the economic factors and motives in history rather than on cultural influences and emphasize the role of class in shaping relations within societies. To these scholars, then, the colonization of Africa was rooted in economic changes and pursuits of the time and the exploitation of Africa also had a class dimension in that African elites participated and emerged in the colonial project as well. A classic work from this perspective is Walter Rodney's *How Europe Underdeveloped Africa*, a popular and powerful survey of the history and impact of African–European relations. Although Marxist scholarship is less prominent today, it was extremely influential throughout the 1970s and into the 1980s by challenging traditional interpretations of colonialism, analyzing the colonial economy and its legacy in postcolonial Africa, and pointing the way to new areas of study for historians.

Over the past three decades, the study of the colonial period has become more nuanced and refined, since historians were able to move beyond the once basic agenda of countering pro-imperialist rhetoric or asserting Africa's place in world history. Moreover, the topics explored and the arguments presented in earlier scholarship raised further questions that needed to be addressed. As a result, the current state of the field of African history is the reverse of what it was at its inception—that is, more scholars specialize in the colonial period and fewer in precolonial African history. The first marked departure from earlier studies of colonialism was the growth of literature focusing on women and gender in colonial Africa, mostly produced by female scholars who were influenced by the women's rights movements of the 1970s. These historians sought not only to recover and highlight women's voices and roles but also to interrogate the part played by gender in colonial society. While today it may seem quite ordinary to study women's history and gender issues, until recently these subjects were largely absent from the historical literature of all areas and time periods of world history.

More recent work on colonialism has investigated a wide spectrum of new topics, including popular culture, gossip and rumor, fashion, medicine and disease, and ecology. In line with the argument that the colonial experience varied greatly from place to place, over time, and among individuals, these studies shed light on how Africans understood, shaped, and remember the colonial period. And while earlier scholarship was primarily regional or continental in scope, historians have since become cognizant of the peculiarities of colonialism in specific places for a variety of reasons, such as culture and environment, and now have a tendency to focus on localized studies. This turn to more narrow topics and locations is a reflection of ideological and theoretical trends in academia and beyond, but it also attests to the achievement of several generations of historians in tackling the difficult work of finding and using sources for the colonial period.

SOURCES ON AFRICA'S COLONIAL HISTORY

From the onset of its establishment as an academic field, historians of Africa have faced many challenges in their work. First and foremost, they had to counter the widespread ignorance and misrepresentation, specifically in the West, of Africa's past. It often seems we continue to fight this battle since lack of knowledge of African history remains pervasive not only within the general public but even within institutions of higher education. Second, they had to reconstruct that past without the benefit of a large body of written documents, the traditional source material for historians. While there are numerous examples of literate societies that produced written documentation, ranging from ancient Egypt in North Africa to the medieval kingdom of Mali in West Africa, most African societies historically tended to privilege oral means of recording their history, customs, and laws. The third challenge, then, was to convince non-Africanists of the usefulness and reliability of oral traditions (among other sources) for reconstructing the past. A pioneer in this effort was Jan Vansina, one of the leading figures of African history, who presented his case and laid out methodological strategies in *Oral Tradition as History*. In the process of confronting these challenges, Africanists not only produced cutting-edge, interdisciplinary scholarship; they also influenced other fields of study. Today most historians of Africa collect, interpret, and discuss a wide range of sources, such as oral history, written documents, linguistic data, and archaeological evidence, in the course of their research.

Writing colonial history, moreover, presents special challenges. In contrast with the pre-colonial period in most of Africa, there is a wealth of written documents produced during colonialism. The authors of these texts, of course, were primarily European colonizers, although many Western-educated African men also generated a written record, including personal letters, newspaper articles, petitions, and scholarly books. Historians always must carefully consider the backgrounds, biases, and agendas of the author of any source material, not just written documents, so naturally these various texts must be understood as reflections of the views of a small group of people who experienced the colonial period, whether as European colonial officials or missionaries, for example, or African elites in the legal or medical field. How, then, do historians find and incorporate the perspectives and experiences of the majority, namely, African women, peasants, workers, and others who were not literate?

The most obvious source is oral history, since there are many Africans (though a decreasing number in much of the continent) who witnessed colonialism firsthand. Scholars differentiate between oral tradition, which refers to events that occurred before one's birth, and oral history, which encompasses one's lifetime. Certainly there are far more people with vivid and comprehensive memories of life under Portuguese rule in a country like Mozambique, which only regained its independence in 1975, than in Libya, where independence from Italy was declared nearly a quarter of a century earlier, in 1951. While historians always must be aware of the challenges presented by oral history, like any source material it allows us to study people's understandings of their own histories, particularly the interpretations of those, such as women, whose voices are often silent in the written historical record. But even written documents can be used to present African voices, as historians have interrogated European colonial records, such as court transcripts, to identify African viewpoints. Social historian Luise White, for example, has shown how African gossip and rumor mentioned in colonial documents help us understand changing colonial policies in East and Central Africa. Thus, by collecting oral history from Africans themselves and reading written records "against the grain," scholars have sought to present African viewpoints on European colonial rule.

OUTLINE OF THE BOOK

In many ways this book is the result of all the aforementioned debates, developments, and challenges, as it represents a synthesis of our current understanding of the colonial period in African history. The pages that follow will explore the colonial period of African history in a thematic and roughly chronological way. Chapter 1 (Economics) focuses on the foundations of colonialism, from the changes taking place in African–European trade during the nineteenth century to the actual conquest and occupation of Africa by Europe through the First World War, an era of outright brutality and plunder. Despite the rhetoric of colonialists, the main motivation for the colonization of

Africa was economic, and Europeans sought to dominate, transform, and develop African economies for their benefit. Nevertheless, Africans were vital actors in these processes, and while some benefited from new opportunities, most suffered the negative consequences of the colonial economy. Chapter 2 (Administration) addresses how the colonial state was organized and how it functioned after the so-called pacification period ended and through the interwar era. Across the continent and over the decades, European colonizers articulated different approaches to administering their colonies, and Africans participated in, commented on, and resisted these experiments. Also explored are the ways in which Africans understood themselves and were perceived by Europeans as well as how their lifestyles, beliefs and practices, and artistic and musical expressions developed under colonial rule. Chapter 3 (Violence) investigates the centrality of violence to colonialism, examining not only how European imperialists used violence to impose and maintain their rule but also the roles that Africans played in such violence in Africa and beyond and how they later employed it in the struggle for independence. Violence could take on many forms, such as the imposition of forced labor or the brutalization of women, but it reached genocidal proportions in the early colonial period in southern and Central Africa. Chapter 4 (Liberation) discusses how Africans won back their freedom and the various ideological influences that shaped anti-colonial movements, including Pan-Africanism, Marxism, and the world religions of Islam and Christianity. The study concludes with some thoughts on the legacy of colonialism by Africans themselves, ranging from Nigerian musician Fela to the Kenyan environmentalist Wangari Muta Maathai.

REFERENCES

Boahen, A. Adu. *UNESCO General History of Africa, volume VII: Africa under Colonial Domination, 1880–1935* (Berkeley: University of California Press, 1990).

Study of the Colonial Period
Allman, Jean, Susan Geiger, and Nakanyike Musisi (eds.). *Women in African Colonial Histories* (Bloomington: Indiana University Press, 2002).

Cooper, Frederick. "Conflict and Connection: Rethinking Colonial African History." *American Historical Review* 99, no. 5 (1994): 1516–1545.

Crowder, Michael (ed.). *West African Resistance: The Military Response to Colonial Occupation* (London: Hutchinson, 1971).

Freund, Bill. "Africanist History and the History of Africa." In *The Making of Contemporary Africa: The Development of African Society since 1800*. Second Edition (Bloomington: Indiana University Press, 1998), 1–13.

Rodney, Walter. *How Europe Underdeveloped Africa*, Revised Edition (Washington, D.C.: Howard University Press, 1982).

Sources on Africa's Colonial History
Vansina, Jan. *Oral Tradition as History* (Madison: University of Wisconsin Press, 1985).

White, Luise. *Speaking with Vampires: Rumor and History in Colonial Africa* (Berkeley: University of California Press, 2000).

Economics

V. I. Lenin, the Russian revolutionary leader and Marxist thinker, famously declared that "imperialism is the highest stage of capitalism." In his pamphlet of the same name, Lenin postulated that European imperialist expansion to places like Africa was the logical result of capitalist growth for three main reasons: domestic consumption in Europe was saturated, so European manufacturers needed new, protected markets abroad for their goods; European capitalists required fresh outlets for investment, and infrastructural development in places like Africa, even if minimal, were regarded as lucrative; and European powers wanted direct, and therefore cheaper, access to tropical raw materials. Lenin presented this thesis during the First World War, nearly twenty years after the so-called Scramble for Africa, as European imperial powers battled each other for global supremacy. While colonial-era propaganda disingenuously claimed that Europe had a responsibility to bring the "Three C's" (Christianity, civilization, and commerce) to Africa, the central assumption of this chapter, following the arguments set forth by Lenin, is that economic motives and factors were the key driving forces for the European conquest of Africa. As economic historian Bill Freund put it, "The imperial conquest of Africa was undertaken to tap African resources in order to help resolve the economic problems of Europe" (*The Making of Contemporary Africa*, 97).

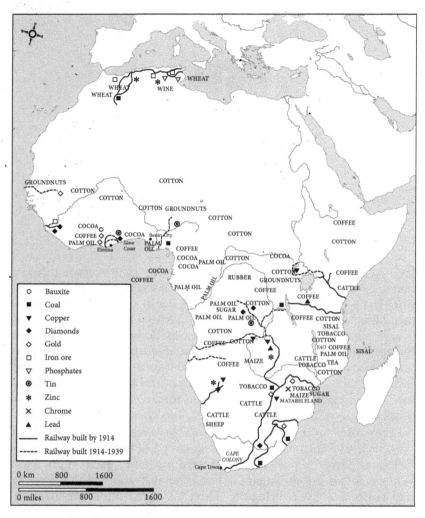

MAP 1 The colonial economy

Many scholars agree that the impetus for colonialism was economic, but other theories have been proposed to explain the Partition of Africa, another phrase used to describe the Scramble. Historians with a Eurocentric focus maintain that the colonization of Africa was merely a side effect of heightened diplomatic confrontations between European states. Along those lines, some identify nationalism as the primary cause, saying that Europeans wanted colonies for prestige and power. Critics of the theory that economics was the prime moti-vating force for colonization point out that African colonies never really attracted significant investment by capitalists. But supporters of Lenin's thesis, Marxist and otherwise, counter by arguing that regard-less of whether investments ended up being substantial, at the time of conquest capitalists were convinced that the colonies would provide protected markets for European manufactured goods, new areas for capitalist investments, and sources of cheap raw materials. Indeed, one of the key features of what has been termed the "New Imperialism" of the late nineteenth century was the capitalist turn from what was called free markets to guaranteed, closed markets, such as those pro-vided by colonies. While both diplomacy and nationalism undoubtedly played a role, these arguments are insufficient to explain the rapidity and totality of the colonial conquest. Proponents of the economic the-sis assert that European diplomatic clashes and nationalist demands for colonies were simply symptoms of the capitalist advance toward imperialism.

As explained in the introduction, relations between Africa and Europe changed drastically in the nineteenth century, partly as a result of technological innovations. For the first time in history Europeans had the upper hand in economic, and increasingly political, interac-tions with Africans. So, what were relations like between Africans and Europeans in the preceding centuries? A common misconcep-tion is that Europeans first journeyed to Africa in the mid–fifteenth century mainly to conquer and enslave. Again, Europeans were in no military position to seize African territory on a significant scale; nei-ther did they necessarily have that impulse before the nineteenth cen-tury. And while the taking of small numbers of slaves did occur, the main reason Europeans sought to establish relations with Africans was for commerce, especially trading for gold. In fact, the very first European structure in sub-Saharan Africa was called Elmina Castle after the Portuguese word for mine. Completed in 1482, it was built along the coast of today's Ghana for easy access to the nearby gold-fields and only with the permission of local rulers who placed strict limits on Portuguese activities there.

Another mistaken belief is that Europeans sold trinkets and other cheap goods to Africans. On the contrary, Portuguese and later European traders often found they had little of value to offer African merchants in exchange for gold. Since West Africa was connected to global trading networks through trans-Saharan routes, luxury goods from far and wide, particularly the Islamic world, were consumed by its elites. Thus Europeans sometimes acted as middlemen in African commerce, securing valuable cloths from Benin City in present-day Nigeria, for instance, to trade for gold in Elmina as per local request. As the Portuguese traveled further afield, rounding the Cape of Good Hope in 1488 and reaching South Asia by the end of the century, their repertoire of trade items was expanded, satisfying African tastes and dispersing goods of varied origin across numerous areas of the Atlantic and Indian oceans.

As the Portuguese, Spanish, and other Europeans conquered and settled the Americas, the nature of African–European trade, particularly in West and Central Africa, changed. By the end of the sixteenth century, Europeans primarily sought to buy human beings from Africans for enslavement in the silver and gold mines and the plantations of sugar, tobacco, cotton, and other crops in the so-called New World. But here too the popular perception of Europeans raiding African villages for slaves is largely false. Slaves were captured in war, sentenced to slavery for judicial or religious offenses, or simply kidnapped by Africans and then sold to European merchants along the coast. In exchange, Africans purchased various goods of European and other origins that circulated in the triangular trade of the Atlantic world, including cloth, firearms, and alcohol, among others, most of which were destined for consumption by the ruling and commercial elites. Some African states at times flourished and expanded as they profited from this trade while other peoples, particularly those in what scholars call "decentralized societies," were devastated and still other groups were virtually untouched by the slave trade. In other words, the effects of the slave trade varied from place to place and within each area could change over time.

Despite the mixed impact of the transatlantic slave trade, relations between African and European states, rulers, and merchants remained mostly peaceful and equal, with some major exceptions, such as in southern Africa where Europeans conquered and colonized Africans as early as the sixteenth century. But, by and large, as stated by Basil Davidson, a celebrated historian of Africa, Europeans were masters of the sea while Africans were masters of the land. In the Americas, of course, the relationship was violent and unequal: Europeans sold, bought, exploited, abused, and killed Africans. All told, scholars estimate that anywhere from nine to fifteen million or more Africans were transported across the Atlantic Ocean to slavery in the New World.

ABOLITION AND "LEGITIMATE COMMERCE"

In the early nineteenth century, attitudes toward slavery abruptly changed in Britain, the foremost slave trader until then, and it took the lead in abolishing the slave trade following a parliamentary act in 1807. Debates about the reasons for this reversal persist, the prevailing argument being that changes in morality rooted in the general philosophical current of the time, the European Enlightenment, along with the Christian Methodist movement, led abolitionists to take up the campaign to end the slave trade. The signature motto of "Am I not a brother?" circled an image of a black man in chains in abolitionist propaganda. While the emphasis in historical literature has been on these European-led campaigns to end the slave trade, slaves also played an important—and perhaps the key—role in abolition. The varied, creative, and subversive ways that slaves resisted, ranging from "passive" acts like refusing to speak the slaveholder's language or practice his religion to such violent forms as armed rebellion, always provoked fear among Europeans in slave societies in the Americas. In 1791, the slaves of Saint-Domingue (present-day Haiti), then France's largest Caribbean colony and a major producer of the world's coffee and sugar, rose up en masse against the small European population. News of the rebellion sent shockwaves across the Atlantic world, frightening European slaveholders and thrilling slaves, as indeed the number of revolts in the United States and elsewhere increased in the ensuing years. After more than a decade of bloodshed and repeated European efforts to suppress the revolution, in 1804 Haiti became the first black republic in the world, only the second independent country in the Americas, and a source of hope and inspiration for the tens of millions of Africans still enslaved across the Americas. The fact that slaves continually resisted their enslavement, and the example of successful rebellions like that in Saint-Domingue and smaller ones elsewhere in the Americas, at least partly served as an impetus for ending the slave trade.

Beyond the ideas of European abolitionists and the actions of African slaves, historians have identified economic changes as a cause leading to the end of the slave trade. In fact, radical scholars argue it is the essential factor that even made the shift in European moral attitudes possible. As capitalism and industrialization intensified in Britain, the material and labor needs of the country changed significantly. Slave labor and its products were no longer as profitable while demand for raw materials—in particular tropical products like palm oil, wild rubber, and ivory—increased considerably. It was more in Britain's interest, therefore, for agricultural production in coastal West Africa to expand than for Britain to remove potential producers of raw materials and consumers of manufactured goods and transport them to the Americas. From this perspective, it is no surprise that Britain, as the most advanced capitalist country, took the lead in ending the slave trade. One of the earliest proponents of this argument, the Trinidadian intellectual and politician Eric Williams, labeled it a "myth" that humanitarian factors rather than economic changes and motives led to the end of the slave trade.

Today the insincerity of Britain, the biggest participant in the slave trade, suddenly deciding it was immoral, might seem obvious, but perhaps even more hypocritical was its use of the term "legitimate trade" to describe its commerce with Africa in the decades following abolition. Despite Britain's efforts, from lobbying other European governments to dispatching naval patrols along the West African coast, the slave trade continued until nearly the end of the nineteenth century. It has been estimated that an additional three million slaves were transported across the Atlantic after Britain's abolition, particularly to Cuba and Brazil, and in East Africa the slave trade actually increased in the 1800s, reaching its height during the first five decades. Most of the African slaves there were destined to distant parts of the Islamic world, but just off the East African coast the island of Zanzibar became an important center of the slave trade as well as slavery on its clove plantations.

As Britain tried to block slave ships from crossing the Atlantic, the slave trade and the use of slaves within West Africa increased. This partly was due to the obvious fact that while slaving continued in the interior, demand at the coast declined as a result of Britain's anti-slaving operations. Concurrently, the reliance on slaves in agriculture expanded within major slave-exporting kingdoms, such as Asante (in today's Ghana) and Dahomey (Benin). While slaves were used in Asante kola nut cultivation for northern markets in the Islamic world, Dahomey employed slave labor on plantations dedicated to palm oil production for export to Europe. Likewise, in the Senegambia region, slaves worked on farms growing groundnuts (peanuts) for European consumption. The oils derived from groundnut and oil palms were used as industrial lubricants as well as in the manufacturing of soap and candles. Slaves marched to the coast and acquired from expansionist wars in the interior thus were employed in cash crop agriculture for the so-called legitimate trade.

West African merchants played a key role in the development of this new commercial relationship with Europe, particularly through financing the expansion of cash crops. As the intermediaries between European traders and African producers and consumers, they recognized the potential profit from investing in export-oriented agriculture as the Atlantic slave trade went into decline. Scholars call this class of men compradores, a term derived from the era when China was under the imperialist yoke of the West and a similar group of local men served as intermediaries there. The West African compradores spoke European languages, often practiced Christianity, were literate, and embraced Western cultural habits yet were intimately connected with local communities, making them ideal middlemen in African–European trade. Although this merchant class existed for several centuries in West Africa, chiefly in those places were the slave trade was most pronounced, their significance was marked during the nineteenth century as European economic and political influence rose in tandem with the intensifying commercial relationship.

INFORMAL COLONIALISM

Historians refer to this period, when the slave trade went into decline and there was a shift toward so-called legitimate commerce, as the era of informal colonialism since European nations began to exert more power in some places and the numbers of European traders, missionaries, and explorers everywhere increased. The latter generally traveled to areas of the continent previously off-limits to Europeans or far beyond their bases in order to compile reports on the geography, economics, and politics of interior states, information that would prove crucial to conquest. Until the mid–nineteenth century, only a few minor coastal territories scattered across the vast African continent were directly controlled by Europeans. The two major exceptions were the long-established British Cape Colony at the southern end of Africa and, in the north, the French colony of Algeria occupied beginning in the 1830s. Both of these were settler colonies, attracting not only migrants from their respective metropoles, or home countries, but other Europeans as well, particularly Germans and Portuguese in Cape Colony and Italians and Spaniards in Algeria. These European settler communities expanded violently in the nineteenth century, displacing African communities, seizing the most arable land, and generally laying the foundation for future conflicts. Another type of settler colony, populated by freed slaves from the Americas and repatriated Africans from slave ships stopped by British naval patrols, developed in West Africa in the first half of the nineteenth century. Although neither attracted European settlers, Sierra Leone, a British colony from 1808, and Liberia, an independent republic in 1847, nevertheless were characterized by colonial-type relations between the settler and indigenous populations. Over the following decades, the extent of territories directly controlled by Europeans grew, yet the number of prosperous and expanding African states increased during the nineteenth century, too, and many areas of the continent experienced an economic boom as result of legitimate trade.

Historians must be careful not to let our knowledge of the past overly influence the way we reconstruct our narratives. Although it is obvious that Europe successfully colonized almost all of Africa by the end of the nineteenth century, for example, the coming of colonial rule was not a foregone conclusion even a few years before the Scramble for Africa. So, while the colonial era may seem to us an inevitable outcome of African-European relations in the mid-1800s, at that time neither Africans nor Europeans foresaw an Africa conquered and occupied by Europeans. A. Adu Boahen, an eminent Ghanaian historian, writes

> The most surprising aspects of the imposition of colonialism on Africa were its suddenness and its unpredictability. By as late as 1880, there were no real signs or indications of this phenomenal and catastrophic event. On the contrary, an overwhelming majority of the states and polities of Africa were enjoying their sovereign existence, and their rulers were in full control of their own affairs and destinies. (*African Perspectives on Colonialism*, 1)

Indeed, Boahen explains that, counter to assumptions that Africa was in crisis on the eve of colonialism, several major transformative processes were under way across Africa throughout the nineteenth century. First, farmers and traders took advantage of the shift to legitimate trade by embracing new crops, expanding production of those in greater demand, and extending local and regional commercial networks to the point that, for the first time in history, trade crossed Central Africa linking the Atlantic and Indian oceans, in what he calls the "commercial unification of Africa" (*African Perspectives on Colonialism*, 5). Second, along with the increase in large, centralized states, the rationalization of political and economic administration, particularly in areas like West Africa where the population included a Western-educated merchant and intellectual class, and the modernization of military organization and materials occurred. Third, Islam and Christianity, along with the literacy and education associated with both religions, spread to more parts of Africa through state expansion, reform movements, and African and European missionary activities. The result in many places was the introduction of religious pluralism as well as the emergence of minorities who constituted literate elites within their societies. Finally, the nineteenth century witnessed the beginnings of Pan-Africanism, first as the intellectual conception of a shared "African Personality" across the continent and the African diaspora in opposition to prevailing European racist notions and later as a political ideology in resistance to European imperialism.

Yet, with the expansion of capitalism across western Europe (as well as the United States, whose imperialism did not extend to Africa, though) and the resultant marked competition for markets and resources, the attraction of African territories became irresistible to European powers. A series of events in the late 1870s presaged the Scramble for Africa associated with the following decade. In many ways the French took the lead by organizing two major explorations, along the trans-Saharan trade routes in West Africa and in the Congo basin in Central Africa, where other European nations, particularly Belgium and Britain in the latter case, also had interests. Additionally, the military conquest and occupation of territory near its small possessions on the Senegalese coast was initiated. In 1883, the French annexed Porto Novo and Little Popo along the so-called Slave Coast in the present-day countries of Benin and Togo, respectively. Determined to check French expansion, the British, the dominant European economic power in Africa, proclaimed protectorates over their coastal possessions in today's Nigeria and Cameroon. The following year, the Germans, who had no colonies until this point but feared missing out on the Scramble, seized West African coastal towns in what is currently Togo and Cameroon after coercion from commercial firms and missionary societies.

It was often these two groups, along with nationalist organizations, that pressured their governments to annex African territories in which they were engaged in economic or religious activities. In fact, missionaries were in many ways the advance guard of colonization, reporting on the economic and political status of the places in which they worked and agitating for European intervention against what they viewed as barbaric African practices. Jomo Kenyatta, the first president of Kenya at independence, succinctly summarized the accessory role of missionaries in a famous quote attributed to him: "When the missionaries arrived, the Africans had the land and the missionaries had the Bible. They taught us how to pray with our eyes closed. When we opened them, they had the land and we had the Bible." Almost always promoting a specific, nationally based denomination of Christianity, these groups—with names like the London Missionary Society, the Rhenish Missionary Society, and the Church Missionary Society—usually operated in the areas where their compatriots predominated in trade and that eventually were colonized by their metropole.

Pushed by varied interests, whatever their particular motives, and sometimes in spite of the obvious lack of immediate economic or political justification, European governments suddenly were gripped by Scramble fever, fearing they would be left out of the race for colonies and the subsequent riches everyone believed it promised if they did not act quickly and decisively.

SCRAMBLE FOR AFRICA

Despite the competitive and sometimes haphazard nature of the initial Scramble, remarkably the European powers avoided armed conflict between each other. Indeed, in order to assure an orderly and peaceful, at least on the European side, seizure of African territories, the German Chancellor Otto von Bismarck convened a meeting of the leading imperialist powers—namely, Britain, France, Germany, Belgium, and Portugal. Delegates from these nations met in the German capital from November 1884 to January 1885 at what was known as the Berlin West Africa Conference, where they created guidelines, without any African participation whatsoever, for dividing the African continent (and not just the western part as the conference name suggests). They agreed to the following rules: the other powers should be notified if any one nation claims African territory so that counterclaims could be resolved; claims would be recognized only when that nation effectively occupied the territory; treaties of protection signed between European representatives and African rulers would be considered legitimate; the Niger and Congo rivers, important trade routes coveted by all the attendees, would remain free zones accessible to all; and, perhaps most significantly for the Scramble and the subsequent borders of Africa, each nation was free to extend its occupation into the interior from any coastal possession. So, contrary to the popular idea that the European powers definitively divided up what King Leopold of Belgium called "this magnificent cake," thus creating the map of colonial Africa at the Berlin Conference, they mainly established the course of action for conquest and occupation.

In other words, the actual partition of Africa followed the conference, as European nations, operating from their various coastal bases across the continent, waged diplomatic and military offensives to take over hitherto sovereign African states and peoples. The methods varied from place to place, depending on local political circumstances, but generally-speaking Europeans knowingly and repeatedly resorted to deception and threats to achieve their primary objective, namely, the signing of "treaties of protection." A typical case took place in 1884 in what is today Togo, where German soldiers kidnapped a number of chiefs from coastal towns, took the African leaders aboard a warship, and forced the chiefs to sign over their territory to the Germans. European agents and explorers usually described these documents to African rulers as friendship agreements, whereby they would offer protection to the signatory from attack by neighboring states and peoples. The fact that some African rulers viewed these treaties as desirable should not be overlooked, as smaller, weaker states often welcomed the offer of protection against powerful, expansionist neighbors. But more commonly, especially when European intentions were more apparent and the African ruler had a powerful military to back him, the treaties of protection were refused, at least for the time being. For instance, a few years after the Togo incident, in 1890, across the continent in present-day Tanzania, the Germans were rebuffed by Machemba, king of the Yao, who bluntly declined an offer of protection, realizing it was a disguised ploy to take over his country. King Machemba boldly told the German commander Hermann von Wissmann:

I have listened to your words but can find no reason why I should obey you—I would rather die first. ... If it should be friendship that you desire, then I am ready for it, today and always; but to be your subject, that I cannot be. ... If it should be war you desire, then I am ready, but never to be your subject. ... I do not fall at your feet, for you are God's creature just as I am ... I am Sultan here in my land. You are Sultan there in yours. Yet listen, I do not say to you that you should obey me; for I know that you are a free man. ... As for me, I will not come to you, and if you are strong enough, then come and fetch me. (*African Perspectives on Colonialism*, 23–24)

In these kinds of interactions, when European officials or representatives generally appeared with a small retinue of soldiers, most often hired African mercenaries, and prepared written documents ready for signature, the show of force and the advantages of literacy each played an important role. Europeans sought to intimidate African rulers with an impressive military demonstration, partly to discourage any thoughts of resistance, and to exploit their monopoly on writing to misrepresent or withhold key aspects of what was being signed. Indeed, while historians emphasize the role of technological innovations of the nineteenth century, such as the steamship and the railway, the power of literacy in the colonization of Africa often is overlooked. Of course there were some literate African rulers or state officials who could read and write for them, but usually signatories of these treaties of protection were at the mercy of the Europeans to explain what they were signing. Sometimes African rulers were deceived by the Europeans they had trusted for advice, as in the case of the famous Rudd concession of 1888, whereby the British imperialist Cecil Rhodes acquired rights to the mineral resources of what became known as Southern Rhodesia (present-day Zimbabwe) after the illiterate king of Matabeleland, Lobengula, was encouraged to sign by his European missionary advisor.

As the European powers collected these treaties across the continent, a series of what has been termed "regional scrambles" ensued, with Britain usually the leading player. Historian John Iliffe likens the partition to a game of chess, as each European nation made claims on territory bordering the claims of others and the swapping of territory in order to avoid conflict and rationalize boundaries, as least from the European perspective, was common (*Africans*, 197). On the African side, states and peoples almost always acted unilaterally, meaning there was little cooperation between neighbors on how to deal with these European officials and representatives touting treaties. In retrospect, it is easy to assume that Africans should have seen the writing on the wall, so to speak, and come together diplomatically and militarily to forge a common position in negotiations with Europeans. And, of course, there were cases of unity in resisting colonization, but for the most part African rulers considered their own interests first and foremost, which explains why some agreed to protection treaties in the face of hostile neighbors.

If we investigate each case on its own, then, we will see that African states and peoples were often conflicted about how to deal with the Europeans and, just as likely, changed tactics depending on the circumstances. The first decision each African ruler had to make was whether to accede to European protection or to reject it. The latter choice, of course, meant that a military conflict was inevitable if the Europeans made threats, so the possibility of success, particularly in view of nearby alliances between other Africans and the colonizing Europeans, had to be carefully considered. Iliffe suggests that officials in individual African states were usually divided between the "doves," those who were willing to agree to European terms, and the "hawks" determined to defend their sovereignty (200). Sometimes, the perspectives were more complex, as in the case of the kingdom of Buganda (in present-day Uganda), where rival Muslim, Catholic, and Protestant factions of the court sought to gain the upper hand in dealing with the British. Likewise, it was not uncommon for an African ruler to sign a treaty of protection and then later renounce the agreement. Other times, African states and peoples requested "protection" after suffering a devastating defeat in resisting European occupation. In the absence of written records of the deliberations taking place in communities across the continent, we only can imagine the heartfelt opinions expressed in the countless debates that took place in chiefly palaces, community meeting places, and family homes.

Readers familiar with Nigerian writer Chinua Achebe's classic *Things Fall Apart* may recognize this process as it played out in the Igbo village depicted in the novel. At first, the European presence is minimal, mainly in the form of goods and ideas introduced into the community following the arrival of some missionaries. The latter are treated with suspicion by most people in the village, and the first Igbo converts to Christianity are people of low status, but slowly others embrace the religion, if only seemingly for access to Western education and other perceived benefits. Meanwhile, officials from a nearby British colonial station begin interfering in the affairs of the community, although the village elders retain power. These events cause divisions in the community, as exemplified by the following exchange between Okonkwo and Obierika, central characters in the book:

"Does the white man understand the custom of our land?"

"How can he when he does not even speak our tongue? But he says that our customs are bad; and our own brothers who have taken up his religion also say that our customs are bad. How do you think we can fight when our own brothers have turned against us? The white man is very clever. He came quietly and peacefully with his religion. We were amused at his foolishness and allowed him to stay. Now he has won our brothers, and our clan can no longer act like one. He has put a knife on the things that held us together and we have fallen apart."

After the nearby murder of a European, the British respond by attacking the village, making a strong impression on many of the residents who now fear European military power. As the influence and authority of the Europeans grow, represented by colonial officials like the district commissioner, some in the village, particularly Okonkwo, call for confronting the British with force. After the mission station is attacked, the British take full control of the village and impose a fine, and this Igbo community loses its sovereignty. This is a fictionalized account of the European takeover of one village, but similar events occurred nearby and far away, as the independence of countless communities, small and large, vanished through European deception and force.

COLONIAL ECONOMY

Nevertheless, the conquest and colonization of Africa was an ongoing, incomplete process, as large areas of the continent remained outside of European control well into the early twentieth century and Africans resisted colonial rule almost everywhere. Some of the wars and rebellions against European occupation will be discussed in chapter 3, but it should be pointed out here that, on the whole, the most difficult places for Europeans to colonize were those where stateless peoples predominated. Significant areas of North Africa where pastoralists resided, such as the Berbers in Morocco and the Bedouin in Libya, and parts of West Africa inhabited by decentralized societies, like the Baoulé of Côte d'Ivoire and the aforementioned Igbo of Nigeria, retained their independence, at considerable human and material costs, for several decades after the Scramble began.

But, for the most part, much of the continent, particularly the coastal areas and immediate hinterlands, effectively was under European control by the turn of the century. Once the Europeans believed the so-called pacification phase was complete, their attention turned to the main agenda of colonial rule, the reorganization of local economies for the benefit of their metropoles. On the whole, this meant a series of complimentary, transformative strategies over time, namely, the introduction or expansion of cash crops and mining; the rationalization of land ownership and use (in the opinion of the colonists); the exclusion of Africans from commerce, especially export–import trade; the redirection of existing (in other words, precolonial) trade routes toward newly established colonial capitals and ports along the

How to reorganize local economies

coasts or elsewhere; the construction and extension of railways and roads from those colonial centers into areas of intensive agriculture, mining, or other export-oriented activities; the introduction of taxes, direct and indirect, and cash wages; and, perhaps most important, the control of African labor, which in some places meant the abolition of slavery, although European colonial officials often were reluctant to upset existing social hierarchies.

We can identify these strategies from our study of the historical record, but it should be emphasized that during the early period of colonial rule there was virtually no centralized planning or coordination but, rather, informal, often private initiatives, especially by European concessionary companies. Indeed, the period was marked more by plunder than anything else, as colonial agents acted like tribute takers, extracting surplus from African producers and ransacking communities that refused to oblige. And, again, the process varied everywhere, depending on local circumstances, not least of all African economic initiatives and resistance to European demands. In fact, even in East Africa, where colonial officials dispossessed the most fertile land for European settler agriculture, African farming was often more productive and profitable to the point where colonial officials in Kenya, for instance, prohibited Africans from growing coffee, tea, · and cotton in order to appease settler demands for African labor. By 1913, three-quarters of Kenya's exports were produced by Africans, and even the percentage generated by European settlers is uncertain, as they often employed small-scale African cultivators on their land.

The conflict between African and European farmers in Kenya attests to the fact that the proliferation of cash crops was not solely the result of imperialist dictates. By and large, African peasants voluntarily grew cash crops and in some cases were the instigators of the introduction and expansion of them, as evidenced by the steady growth of various crops for export in the decades before colonization. The most famous case is the cultivation in the Gold Coast (now Ghana) of cocoa, a crop that became synonymous with the colony during the colonial era (and remains the top earner for Ghana today), which was the initiative of African farmers, not European administrators. There are conflicting accounts of the introduction of the American plant to Ghana, attributed either to Swiss missionaries or more popularly to a local farmer named Tetteh Quarshie, but the crop was so successful in the soil and climate of the Gold Coast and so profitable to its cultivators that cocoa was enthusiastically planted throughout the colony.

Women in the Gold Coast carrying bales of cocoa for export, circa 1900. African farmers had initiated the cultivation of cocoa in the late precolonial period, and its expansion was encouraged by British colonial officials. Cocoa remains Ghana's primary export, a legacy of the colonial era emphasis on cash crops. Basel Mission archives.

On the other hand, Africans resisted growing cash crops that were time-consuming and detrimental to other agricultural pursuits, as in the case of cotton. Moreover, if the benefits of cash crop farming were not forthcoming, such as when the prices proffered by colonial regimes were below the prevailing rates, African farmers abandoned their cultivation or else diverted their produce outside the colonial economy. In German Togoland, for instance, cotton was sent north on trade routes that linked up to the trans-Saharan network rather than south to the colonial port at Lomé since prices offered by traveling Hausa merchants were higher than those of the Germans. This is one of numerous examples from across the continent of the resilience on pre-colonial economic systems despite the European military and political conquest of Africans states and peoples, although the construction of railways in the following years eventually displaced many of these older trading networks. This subversion of the colonial economic system infuriated the German regime, which struck back with edicts, punishments, and cotton-growing schemes all aimed at forcing African farmers to cultivate cotton for the German market.

The German quest for cotton exemplifies the primary objective of European imperialism in Africa, namely, the creation of colonies as specialized producers for the home countries and, to a larger extent, the global capitalist economy. For Germany, which was dependent on cotton exports from the United States, its Togoland colony promised a guaranteed source for its domestic textile industry. Although cotton was cultivated in West Africa, including the area of German Togoland, for centuries before European occupation, German colonial officials, like their counterparts across Africa, assumed that African farmers needed to be taught more efficient and effective agricultural methods. The local practice of what is called slash-and-burn agriculture, whereby plots are weeded and prepared for cultivation through controlled burning, was banned by the Germans, who considered it counterproductive and illogical. African farmers knew from experience that the technique successfully destroyed poisonous plants and enriched the iron-poor soils of the area, but they faced fines or flogging if they violated this colonial ban. Moreover, the German effort to introduce what they perceived to be progressive agricultural practices and to encourage the expansion of cash crops went beyond unpopular administrative edicts to the pursuit of a transnational cotton-growing scheme.

After roughly a decade of German military campaigns to occupy central Togoland, the effort to expand and improve cotton cultivation was kick-started through a complex and curious alliance between German and white American academics, the African American leader Booker T. Washington, and German colonial administrators. The strange story of the so-called Tuskegee Expedition, named after Washington's teaching and research institute in the United States, is laid out in detail in historian Andrew Zimmerman's aptly named book *Alabama in Africa*. In addition to establishing an experimental cotton farm and a cotton-growing school, the four African American men who arrived in German Togoland in January 1901 were charged with promoting what colonialists considered the ideal productive unit: a patriarchal, monogamous family working a small farm. In so doing, colonial officials hoped not only to replicate the stereotyped docile, hardworking "negro" of the American south in Togoland, but also to transform local marriage and family arrangements that encouraged the relative economic independence of women and a migratory kind of commerce, both of which were non-conducive to colonial labor demands. The expedition was a mixed success, as its leader, John W. Robinson, died in a drowning accident in 1909, yet the farm and school remain in operation as agricultural research stations in present-day Togo.

While the particular circumstances and unusual group of actors in the Tuskegee Expedition make it unique, in many ways the aims of the project were typical of European imperialism in Africa. In other words, besides promoting cash crops and other commodities to benefit the home countries, colonial administrators sought to transform African social institutions in support of their economic agenda. In fact, scholars argue that the ultimate objective of European imperialists in Africa, creating efficient, self-financing, commodity-producing colonies for the metropoles, was a long-term process requiring investment, personnel, and time.

The introduction of taxes, direct and indirect, was another component of this long-term strategy. Revenues collected from Africans financed colonial administration and infrastructural development, since colonies were expected to be self-sufficient and subsidies from the metropole were limited. Taxation also forced Africans into wage labor, the only means of obtaining European currency, thus providing cheap labor for infrastructural projects and European settler farms, two of the major exploiters of African workers. All kinds of taxes were levied on Africans, the best known being the so-called hut tax and the poll tax, and new ones were created to bolster colonial state coffers. The example of German Togoland is apropos again, as the taxes imposed on Africans in the colony were extensive and absurd. At one point, chiefs were required to fly the German flag on their homes, after which a tax on flying the German flag was levied! The burden of paying taxes was so great that many Africans simply migrated to the neighboring Gold Coast to avoid labor conscription. Indeed, forced labor was used throughout colonial Africa as a punishment for not paying taxes, and African men often were sent far from their homes for extended periods working on infrastructural projects, such as the building of roads and railways, where conditions were horrendous and the injury and death tolls high.

The construction of railways from the coasts to the cash crop zones or mining areas in the interior was another of the key factors in the development of the colonial economy. The impact of railways was dramatic: they significantly reduced transport time and costs and, as a result, supplanted precolonial trade networks; new towns arose and existing ones expanded along their routes; railways expedited and promoted travel, migration, and urbanization; and they facilitated the exploitation of Africa's vast mineral resources. Indeed, besides such cash crops as oil-producing nuts and kernels, cotton, sisal, cocoa, coffee, and tea, Africa's mineral resources were the main prize for European imperialists. Gold Coast gold, Nigerian tin, Congolese copper, and Tunisian phosphates all held promise, but the greatest mineral wealth, primarily in the form of gold, was initially found in southern Africa. As mentioned previously, European colonization in that part of the continent occurred long before the Scramble, beginning with the establishment of a small Dutch base at Cape Town in 1652. The European settler population of diverse origins grew and developed a distinct dialect of Dutch called Afrikaans, which also incorporated aspects of other languages, including Khoikhoi spoken by the pastoralists who dominated the area before European colonization. The Afrikaners, as they preferred to be known instead of the somewhat derogatory term Boers, predominated in a colonial society that also included free and enslaved Africans and slaves imported from South Asia and that expanded their settlements outside the Cape often by force.

By the early nineteenth century, the Cape Colony was taken over by the British, who attempted to abolish slavery, transform the local economy, and expand and secure the colonial frontiers with neighboring African states and peoples. Resistant to British rule and frustrated by limited access to land and labor, in 1834 the Afrikaners embarked on what they termed the Great Trek, a migration of about 10,000 to areas northeast of the colony that eventually became known in the 1860s as the South African Republic. By this time, the southern tip of Africa was a complex array of European colonial (British) and settler (Afrikaner) territories comprising a significant mixed population of African, European, and Asian ancestries and independent and semi-independent African states. The discovery of gold in the Afrikaner-ruled South African Republic in 1886, however, facilitated the expansion and consolidation of British colonial rule over the entirety of southern Africa. The quintessential imperialist schemer, Cecil Rhodes, who served as a British colonial official at the Cape, negotiated treaties with African rulers throughout southern Africa, and invested heavily in the newly discovered diamond and gold finds, was one of the primary instigators of conflict between the British and the Afrikaners, which culminated in the bloody and costly South African

War of 1889–1902. The British victory not only consolidated its control of southern African territory and wealth but, most significantly, its domination of the world supply of gold.

In addition to the extraction of commodities like cash crops and minerals, the developing colonial economies throughout Africa shared other features. First, European monopoly firms like Comagnie française de l'Afrique occidentale in French West Africa and Unilever in British West Africa largely controlled the export of African raw materials and the import of European manufactured goods. Second, a class of merchants of foreign origin, including Indians, Lebanese, and Greeks, generally served as middlemen between African producers and consumers and the European trading firms. Third and last, Africans migrated in search of work to centers of cash crop and mining production, such as the cocoa belt in Côte d'voire and the Gold Coast, the groundnut zone in the Senegambia, the cotton-growing areas of Sudan and Uganda, and the mines of South Africa, Belgian Congo, and Northern Rhodesia.

CONCLUSION

What we today identity as the early colonial period ended with the First World War, then known as the Great War, fought mostly between European imperial powers but, as will be shown in chapter 3, involving hundreds of thousands of Africans as well. The early colonial period therefore was marked by the conquest and occupation of African territories; the coerced and voluntary incorporation of African farmers and laborers into commodity production; the emergence of three different kinds of cash crop production by African farmers, European settlers, and African peasants on European-owned plantations; the development of key mining areas, particularly in southern and Central Africa; and the construction of a basic infrastructure to deliver commodities from the interior to the coast. By the end of the First World War, when the map of colonial Africa was re-drawn by the Allies to dispossess Germany of its African territories, European colonial administrators recognized that concessionary company rule had to be replaced with more formal state institutions and policies to more effectively exploit the human and material resources of Africa.

REFERENCES

Freund, Bill. "The Material Basis of Colonial Society, 1900-40." In *The Making of Contemporary Africa: The Development of African Society since 1800.* Second Edition (Bloomington: Indiana University Press, 1998), 97–124.

Lenin, V. I, *Imperialism: The Highest Stage of Capitalism* (New York: International Publishers, 1939).

Abolition and "Legitimate Commerce"
Williams, Eric. *Capitalism and Slavery* (Chapel Hill: University of North Carolina Press, 1944).

Informal Colonialism
Boahen, A. Adu. *African Perspectives on Colonialism* (Baltimore, Md.: Johns Hopkins University Press, 1987).

Scramble for Africa
Achebe, Chinua. *Things Fall Apart* (New York: Anchor Books, 1994).

Iliffe, John. *Africans: The History of a Continent* (New York: Cambridge University Press, 1995).

Colonial Economy
Zimmerman, Andrew. *Alabama in Africa: Booker T. Washington, the German Empire, and the Globalization of the New South* (Princeton, N.J.: Princeton University Press, 2010).

Administration

A popular field of study among an earlier generation of scholars was comparative colonialism, which contrasted different systems of European colonial rule in Africa. The premise was that we could learn about the nature and impact of colonial rule by comparing the distinct ways Europeans ruled Africa. It is common for historians of Africa to be asked, "Who were the worst colonizers?" implying that some imperialists were better than others. While most Africanists agree that European colonial rule in general was exploitative, violent, and indisputably illegal, they also recognize there were subtle and sometimes major distinctions in the administration of colonies, though it is not possible to designate one European imperial power as better than the other. Furthermore, we can distinguish between two very different kinds of colonies in Africa, settler and nonsettler, meaning those with a significant European settler population (mainly located in North, East, and southern Africa) and those without. Just as important, there was considerable economic disparity within individual colonies, often between a more developed geographic area of commodity production and an undeveloped part that functioned mainly as a source of migrant laborers. Therefore, while we can identify general aspects of colonial administration, its implementation and effects varied from colony to colony and within each colony.

As discussed in the previous chapter, European colonial powers did not articulate or implement coherent, deliberate plans for

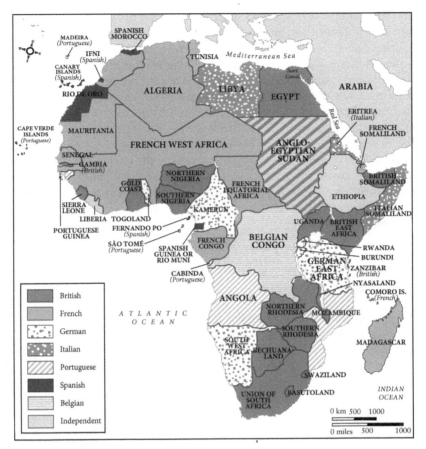

MAP 2   Colonial boundaries in 1914

administering their new African colonies in the early colonial period. Instead, whatever governance was in place was carried out by concessionary companies or other private enterprises or negligible colonial administration. While this was a cheap way to somehow manage colonies, the negative ramifications for the lives of Africans as well as the public image of European governments were apparent, as exemplified by the mass killings in Belgian king Leopold's Congo Free State, a topic to be covered in chapter 3. In essence, concessionary companies were first and foremost concerned with maximizing profit, so any administrative policies they pursued only facilitated that absolute goal. Of course, the more formalized, orderly colonial administration that replaced concessionary company rule also served primarily to make the colonies profitable by exploiting African human and material resources, but they sought to provide at least minimal social services, such as education and health care, which hitherto had been offered only by missionaries in a very limited way. This chapter explores how the European powers administered their colonies in Africa and how the various systems of rule differed as well as the roles Africans played in colonial governance and how they shaped colonial rule. Moreover, it explores how African identities and cultures were transformed during the interwar period, a time of migration, religious innovation, and new social formations.

DISTRICT OFFICERS, INTERMEDIARIES, AND MISSIONARIES

While top European colonial officials and their superiors in the metropoles debated the most effective ways to govern African colonies, the district officer was the everyday face of colonial administration on the ground. District officers were men of various backgrounds who most often were assigned to remote outposts and provided with a scant budget, a few African assistants, and an impossible mandate: to administer a large territory usually comprising many different communities. Although many Africans never met the district officer in person, they certainly knew his local nickname, and usually he was the only contact their chiefs had with the colonial administration based in a far-away capital. While this discussion suggests a tidy system of governance, it must be emphasized that it nearly universally was considered illegitimate by Africans, who viewed district officers as interlopers who usurped their genuine leaders and represented the imposition of alien rule. And despite the common notion that the colonial administration was dominant and effectual, in many areas it was weak or even non-existent. As theorist Ranajit Guha has argued, colonialism was dominance without hegemony, meaning that the colonial administration may have subjugated African economic and political life, but it did not have control over Africans who continued to live their lives in their own ways as much as possible (Cooper, "Conflict and Connection," 1531).

A colonial-era photograph of a district station in the French Congo, circa 1905. District officers in the French colonial system of direct rule were responsible for administrating vast areas comprised of diverse communities. In an effort to discourage their immersion in local culture, these officials were regularly transferred to new postings.

Individual European colonial officials often figure prominently in oral histories of the colonial period. Sometimes these Europeans are well-remembered, since they were posted to a nearby station for a considerable number of years, other times because they were brutal, and less often in recognition of positive contributions they made to local communities. One common feature of these recollections is that the colonial officials are usually not recalled by their proper name but, rather, by a local nickname referring to a physical trait or favorite activity that has preserved in the oral history. These nicknames range from "the Flogger" (or one who whips) in today's Zambia to "Big Belly" in Ghana. In part, this reflects the tendency of oral historians to add humor and animation to recollections, but it also demonstrates the passive ways in which Africans resisted colonialism. Outside the hearing of Europeans, on forced marches to carry their goods, or even right in from of them in a language they did not understand, Africans would mock their supposed superiors by referring to European colonial officials by derogatory names. Europeans also were ridiculed in song, dance, and art, all of which served as outlets to criticize particular colonial policies.

Nevertheless, the district officers who represented the colonial administration in far-flung posts across Africa were in many respects little dictators. In the early colonial period, they tended to be men with a military background who lacked advanced education. Invested with nearly unlimited power and autonomy by colonial regimes, they were responsible for maintaining order, collecting taxes, organizing labor, and administering a mixture of European and what colonial officials termed "native" justice. Yet, since they were placed far and wide, and charged with jurisdiction over a vast territory (mainly because European governments tried to keep administrative expenses as low as possible), colonial regimes relied on African civil servants, often called "African agents" in the historical literature, to carry out their policies and maintain order. These agents were employed as clerks, interpreters, messengers, and soldiers. Quite often, they were alien to the place where they were posted, a deliberate colonial strategy to prevent agents from possibly developing sympathy for the local population. These agents regularly wielded considerable power, if mainly because of their language skills, since they served as the official translators between Africans and European colonial officials. It was not uncommon for an African agent to unilaterally decide who would be granted an audience with the European district officer or, more extremely, what grievances would be forwarded to him. As expected, a considerable level of corruption existed, but the power also could be wielded the other way, as when African agents undermined their European supervisors to the benefit of a particular party, whether an individual, a community, or an entire ethnic group. Classified as collaborators in early studies of the colonial period, some of these agents are now characterized by historians as modernizers who took advantage of colonial institutions and ideologies in order to enhance the economic and political position of their community within the colonial state and in relation to their neighbors. Considering the potential power and influence these African men possessed, it is not surprising that recent scholarship has described them as intermediaries in the colonial system rather than simply as agents of the colonial state. As will be shown, many of these men took the initiative to collect and document local language, history, and culture, often in tandem with European missionaries.

As suggested in the previous chapter, European missionaries were instrumental in the colonization of Africa, not only as outright advocates of imperialism but also as local experts on economic and political conditions on the ground. While individual missionaries sincerely may have believed they were "saving" Africans by introducing them to the Christian religion and European culture, undoubtedly missionaries benefited from colonization since they were able to consolidate and expand their activities in conquered territories. The imperial powers also relied on missionary organizations to provide the minimal education necessary to train a cadre of literate African civil servants for the colonial administration. As Kenyan historian Vincent B. Khapoya rightly concluded, "The relationship between the missions and the colonial governments was truly a symbiotic one" (*The African Experience*, 111). The mission schools, as they were called, also produced African missionaries who played a far larger proselytizing role than did their European teachers with whom they translated the Christian bible into African languages. The curriculum of the schools was focused on basic reading and writing skills with an emphasis on Christian theology and at times was supplemented with training in agriculture or crafts, such as carpentry. Education for women was restricted to domestic skills, such as cooking, sewing, child care, and hygiene, in preparation for the missionary ideal of a Christian marriage, namely, a patriarchal, monogamous relationship with a Christian African man.

The benefits of literacy and Western education, even if limited to low-ranking positions in the bureaucracy and other semi-skilled jobs in the colonial economy, were so attractive that Africans appealed for more educational opportunities. Most Africans had access only to primary education, with very few secondary school options, and a very negligible number were able to complete university studies in Europe or the United States. When educational preferences were not forthcoming, Africans took matters into their own hands to get the training they wanted. Before the First World War, Ewe people in German Togoland simply slipped across the colonial border to the Gold Coast in order to attend mission schools where instruction was in English since knowledge of that language rather than German had more economic potential. In Kenya, Kikuyu communities established their own schools, numbering in the hundreds, because they found the curriculum of the Anglican and Scottish mission schools too limited. While the colonial regimes generally disapproved of these African initiatives, and though they relied on the mission schools to produce literate African workers, financial support usually was not forthcoming, as, particularly in the early colonial period, most missionary societies funded their own schools. After the turmoil of the First World War receded, however, the colonial powers, especially Britain and France, increased investments in education as well as health care and developed and implemented more consistent policies of colonial rule. For instance, in the 1920s British colonial administrations provided limited financial support to and supervision of mission schools.

MODELS OF COLONIAL RULE

The decade following the First World War was characterized by changes in colonial administration and rhetoric. For example, the British were determined to improve colonial administration, principally at the district level by appointing better educated European officers and more efficient and reliable African chiefs. This approach coincided with relative economic prosperity, rapid population growth, and new infrastructural development. In terms of the latter, the introduction of lorries (or trucks) and the expansion of road building had a significant impact on commodity-producing areas and linked communities, particularly in the reduction of transportation costs and time. While there were occasional strikes and boycotts, the large-scale rebellions and armed resistance commonplace in the early colonial period were virtually nonexistent after the First World War. In short, pacification was largely successful, the colonial presence was well-established in most of Africa, and the European powers now were in a position to formalize their colonial administrations.

As the two most significant colonial powers in Africa, not least in terms of territorial control, the British and the French exerted considerable influence on other European nations in the administration of African colonies. After the First World War, Britain and France controlled nearly three-quarters of colonial Africa. While we always must emphasize national, regional, and chronological variations, two general models of colonial administration—French direct rule and British indirect rule—prevailed in the interwar period. The direct model developed somewhat earlier, in the early years of the twentieth century, and was practiced by the Belgians, Portuguese, and French but was most closely associated with the latter. In essence, direct rule meant that Africans would be governed by European administrators who were charged with modernizing their districts through various economic, political, and social means. Since the French model predominated, and affected the largest number of Africans within the direct rule group of colonial powers, the description presented here draws from their approach.

French district officers usually were not based in a particular place for an extended period but instead were assigned new postings on a regular basis. Rather than immerse himself in the study of local cultures and the development of relations with African chiefs, the French official was charged with ruling any one district the same way as any other. Thus, direct rule was a very centralized system in which local variations mattered little in the general application of colonial administration. Despite the name, direct rule functioned only with the support and participation of Africans, particularly chiefs, who were responsible for implementing orders on the ground since there were so few French district officers stationed in vast colonial territories. The French divided their colonies into administrative units, or *cercles*, each headed by a chief, neither of which were legitimate in the opinion of the local population. In other words, cercles did not necessarily reflect precolonial political boundaries but were dictated by French ideas about effective and efficient administration of immense territories, and the selection of chiefs was not based on any local authority. Many times chiefs were not appointed to their home regions, but to distant posts to further accentuate the bureaucratic nature of French colonial rule, even at the level of chief. Rarely did French district officers visit African chiefs in their cercles, as French protocol required chiefs to travel to meet with their French superiors.

One of the responsibilities of chiefs in the French system was to round up possible conscripts for visiting French medical doctors and army officers on annual recruitment drives for the colonial army. Oral history from Senegal informs us that when young men targeted for inspection ran away to avoid conscription, their fathers would be arrested until they returned. The direct rule approach was implemented throughout France's African colonies with some extraordinary exceptions, such as among the Mossi in Upper Volta (present-day Burkina Faso) and in Muslim areas of northern Cameroon, where local rulers continued to exert power, though obviously reduced, during the colonial period.

The system of indirect rule, most closely associated with the British colonial official Lord Frederick Lugard who penned a book on the subject, was the more influential of the two approaches, becoming a model for other colonial powers in the 1930s. In essence, indirect rule meant administering Africans through their own leaders, such as chiefs and sultans. It was assumed that this would not only be more cost-effective but would also lend more legitimacy to the colonial administration in the eyes of Africans. In many ways, the indirect rule approach developed out of the frustration that earlier British colonial officials had felt in not being able to transform African societies to the benefit of the colonial state, so it was hoped that local African rulers, in exchange for such incentives as a modest discretionary budget and a small armed militia, would be willing accomplices in implementing colonial rule.

For the most part, and in contrast to French direct rule, African chiefs retained much of their power, though limited to local affairs, in the British system and tended to preside over the political boundaries that predated colonialism. Furthermore, they were encouraged to apply precolonial laws in the settling of minor judicial matters. Despite the considerable authority local chiefs enjoyed in the indirect rule model, they were nonetheless supervised by British district officers or, rather, were "advised" in the language of British officials, who often introduced changes to customary law, the official term for what were considered as traditional legal codes. Whereas in the early colonial period British district officers often came from military backgrounds, generally were not well-educated, and lacked knowledge of the places they administered, the British made a concerted effort after the First World War to improve the quality of colonial officials.

As a result, British district officers often were posted to a particular area for an extended period and encouraged to learn the prevailing local language and customs. In effect, because the latter were allowed to determine the nature of rule, British administration varied from place to place just as customary laws differed.

IDENTITY AND POLITICS

Indirect rule required an academic component, since British colonial officials sought to understand African traditions and customs in order to employ them in the service of the colonial state. European colonial officials and anthropologists as well as African intermediaries thus collected local histories in an effort to catalog groups of people's history and culture. In the process, political units became tribes, an anthropological term that is still closely associated with Africa regardless of its imprecise usage. In essence, this project of identifying and labeling tribes (or what today are more accurately called ethnic groups) was purely to facilitate administration so that colonial officials could "make sense" of what they perceived to be the myriad linguistic, cultural, religious, and kin groups inhabiting each colony. This drive for order even resulted in tribes being invented where they did not exist, meaning that sometimes groups of people who were culturally or otherwise united in precolonial times were now divided by ethnographers into distinct tribes or, conversely, those previously separate were grouped together. Likewise, where chieftaincy was nonexistent on the eve of colonial rule, chiefs were then created, the most famous case being the imposition of warrant chiefs among the Igbo in southeastern Nigeria. Africans played a major, and sometimes the leading, role in this process by producing definitive ethnographies of their own peoples, thus positioning themselves as experts on laws and customs and perhaps privileging particular lineages, communities, or perspectives as a result. The African authors of these ethnographies, furthermore, were often Western-educated elites who shared some of the worldview of European colonialists, principally the Christian religion. A notable example is the construction of a shared Ewe identity among the various Ewe-speaking peoples of the Gold Coast, Togo, and Dahomey (present-day Benin) that ultimately transformed into nationalist movements for independence and reunification.

As importantly, ordinary Africans, especially migrant workers to urban centers, helped form and shape tribal identities as a way of surviving the colonial economy of cities. When migrants showed up in a big, diverse, unfamiliar city, a far cry from their small, close-knit, rural village, they could rely on members of their own tribe for support and guidance finding accommodation and employment. The various groups that emerged in urban centers, such as tribal associations, thus served to solidify and promote tribal identity. This does not mean that those identities were not legitimate, as indeed Africans often associated language with identity before colonial rule and the urbanization that came with it, but tribal identity, for lack of a better term, was one of many an individual African could claim in the precolonial period. An African could identify with such institutions as lineage, clan, and occupational caste, among others, but the point is that, as a result of African initiative and European policy, the tribal identity became first and foremost during the colonial period. This development certainly had negative ramifications, such as the inability (at least in the short-term) for Africans across a colony to identify with one another against European colonial rule, the hallmark of the European colonial tactic of divide and rule, most extremely witnessed in the stark division of

Rwandans and Burundians into Hutu and Tutsi, which scholars argue became the foundation for mass killings in the postcolonial period.

There were important exceptions, of course, such as the National Congress of British West Africa, established in 1920 by African doctors and lawyers of varied ethnic backgrounds, and the East Africa Association, founded the following year by the Kenyan clerk Harry Thuku. Educated in mission schools and a veteran of the First World War, Thuku employed the knowledge and skills he acquired within the colonial system to protest colonial policies, like his contemporaries in West Africa and elsewhere. In many ways, Thuku was ahead of his time, however, since his concerns extended beyond his own ethnic group, social class, and colony as he sought to rally Africans throughout the British East African colonies, agitation that led to eight years of imprisonment. In his autobiography, published after Kenya's independence, Thuku recalled the development of his political consciousness after the war:

First there were many thousands of porters who came back from very very difficult conditions in the East Africa campaign, and found that they would not get any gratuity. Instead the government under General [Edward] Northey [British governor of Kenya] decided that the white soldiers, and especially the officers, should be rewarded. So they alienated many thousands of acres in the area round Kericho for a Soldier Settlement Scheme....

The second thing that was making Africans angrier after the War was this thing called kipande. This was Swahili for a container in which a registration paper was carried. ... First of all you had to wear this quite heavy metal box round your neck in a string all the time; then in the columns of the paper inside there were many things that were against Africans. There was one place where the employer had to sign when he engaged you and also when you left. ... Another thing in the early kind of kipande was a space for remarks; and here, if an employer did not like you, he could spoil your name completely by putting "lazy," "disobedient," or "cheeky." That column made me very angry. ...

There was also the question of rising taxes for Africans. It kept going up even though we did not see anything like schools or clinics which we get nowadays for our high taxes. The reason for it was to pull African workers out of their houses to work for the European settlers; you see, they could not get the money to pay their taxes unless they left their homes and worked for some months....

I began to have discussions with my friends. We saw clearly that if we sent anything coming from the Kikuyu tribe alone, we would carry no weight. But if we could show that it came from all the tribes—the Maasai, the Kamba etc.,—then we should have a great voice. (*Harry Thuku: An Autobiography*, 18–22)

Despite these early attempts to organize across ethnic lines, most social and political organizations at this time were associated with a particular tribal identity. Nevertheless, migration and urbanization resulted in the creation of dynamic cultural forms and expressions that eventually became politicized as well. One of the best known urban groups was the Beni dance societies, which originated in the early colonial period in Swahili-speaking communities in German East Africa. Characterized by military band music and drills, they became an urban phenomenon, spreading across East and Central Africa following the First World War. African migrants also formed football clubs along tribal lines, initially for recreational purposes, but over time these too became politicized. These various groups helped African migrants survive the harshness of urban life and maintain a link to their rural communities. On a more practical level, the tribal associations in urban centers provided members with important services, such as burial arrangements and academic scholarships.

Migrants often introduced new ideas and technologies to their rural communities, especially religious beliefs and practices as well as anticolonial political consciousness. As more Africans embraced Christianity, new teachings and denominations based on the religion sprang up across the continent. In many ways, these were often a manifestation of opposition to colonial rule in general but more specifically an expression of African understanding of Christianity. To many Africans, the inequality, segregation, and racism of European colonialism, especially when supported by European missionaries, contradicted the lessons of the Christian bible. As a result, many Africans broke away from the missionary churches to establish their own places of worship. Moreover, these independent African churches, as they are called in the historical literature, especially attracted the young and women who felt constrained not only by European Christian dogma but also by the conservative ethos of their traditional rulers and elders. The so-called Ethiopian church and the Zionist churches, both of which originated in South Africa in the late nineteenth century, also emphasized spiritual aspects of worship as opposed to the more rigid services of the missionary churches. Although these independent churches generally did not initiate or encourage militant anticolonial activism, their very existence and their alternative interpretation of Christianity symbolized opposition to European domination. Nonetheless, some of these independent religious organizations did develop into anticolonial movements. The most famous is the church founded in the Belgian Congo in 1921 by Simon Kimbangu, who claimed to be a prophet able to perform miracles. He also preached that god would soon free the Congolese from colonial oppression. He was imprisoned for thirty years by Belgian colonial officials, but Kimbanguism, as it was called, spread, and its adherents refused to pay taxes and grow cash crops in opposition to Belgian rule.

Despite the growth of Christianity, missionary-led and independent, Islam remained the dominant faith for many Africans, particularly in the north and west, and continued to expand as well. Outside of Muslim populations in the northern parts of their West African colonies and along the Indian Ocean coastline, the British ruled a smaller percentage of the African Islamic population than did their French imperial rivals. After initial concerns about the influence of Islam, particularly since the leaders of many of the prominent wars against French colonization invoked the Islamic concept of jihad (self-defense) to rally their troops, in the early colonial period the French developed a less confrontational attitude toward the religion. Indeed, the French colonial state often discouraged Christian missionary activity in predominantly Muslim areas and, in contrast to the British, barely supported European missionaries elsewhere. As a result, Islam actually expanded under French rule, possibly as a form of resistance, and Islamic brotherhoods in North and West Africa, such as the Salafiyya movement based in Egypt, established their own independent schools.

Perhaps the most important organizations to emerge in urban centers, specifically in relation to anticolonial politics, were trade unions. The earliest labor groups formed in the administrative and transport sectors of the colonial economy, in other words among semi-skilled and skilled African workers. Railway employees in Egypt, Sudan, and the Gold Coast, for example, were among the earliest unionized workers, as were dockworkers in East Africa. Although they were small and thus relatively weak, trade unions occasionally went on strike, particularly during the Great Depression.

The 1930s was a contradictory decade for colonial Africa: while the worldwide capitalist depression led to even more repression and exploitation by the European powers, cities grew, mining centers prospered, and colonial administrations provided more access to education and health care in many parts of the continent. In fact, generally speaking, colonial officials emphasized what they considered to constitute economic and social development beginning in the 1930s. During this decade, colonial officials began to invest more resources in public health, particularly hygiene, and opened dispensaries in rural areas, a contrast to the early colonial period, when limited health care was provided mainly by missionaries. The emphasis in colonial medicine was on eradicating epidemic diseases, such as small pox and sleeping sickness. While vaccination campaigns and other public health measures did result in a significant decline of both, colonial medical officers were often heavy-handed providers. In many cases Africans resisted colonial public health campaigns, sometimes rightly concluding that so-called vaccinations were in fact fatal. Rumors in eastern Africa of African vampires who worked with European colonial officials reflected popular fears about colonial medicine. Recent scholarship has investigated how the colonial state also sought to control women's sexuality and reproduction through public health programs. For instance, colonial medical officers and missionaries sought to end female excision and encourage hospital births. While to readers these may appear to be positive goals, the campaigns upset existing social relations, especially the authority of female elders, and therefore generated opposition from affected communities.

In terms of economic developments in the 1930s, the copperbelt of Northern Rhodesia, situated near the other mining center of Katanga in the Belgian Congo, was one of the primary areas of growth in Africa. Africans from throughout Central Africa, including from what were termed Native Reserves, migrated to the copperbelt for work in the mines. At first, conditions in mine camps were appalling—over-crowded, strictly regimented, and lacking in basic social services. Migrant workers left behind their families in the equally horrendous reserves. But as the migrant population grew and the profitably of the mines increased, living conditions improved; families sometimes resided together, some health care and education was provided, and bustling African communities in the urban centers provided economic opportunities and generated new social organizations and cultural forms. Nevertheless, like mines elsewhere in colonial Africa, labor conditions were terrible, with accidents and fatalities being common occurrences. And even though some rural communities prospered, such as the Tonga farmers who provided the mining centers with maize (corn), the migration of large numbers of young men to the urban centers had obvious negative consequences.

Outside of restricted areas of economic growth, however, the Great Depression led to heightened exploitation of African labor and resources. Although Africans faced the shortages and unemployment characteristic of the depression in the rest of the world, European colonial officials raised taxes and relied even more on forced labor. The depression witnessed resistance to colonial rule in many forms: strikes by unionized workers, revolts in rural communities, and urban tax protests. In the recent book *Colonial Meltdown*, Nigerian historian Moses E. Ochonu argues that Africans in one district in northern Nigeria successfully undermined the efforts of British colonial officials to more intensively exploit them to cushion the effects of the depression in Britain. His thesis contradicts the prevailing notion that "nothing [except exploitation] happened" during the depression era by showing how Africans were able to remove themselves from the colonial economy and resurrect or create their own economic activities and strategies, despite the unrelenting demands of the colonial state. The latter accelerated and deepened in the late 1930s, as the Second World War began in Europe, once again drawing Africans into a conflict initiated and mostly fought by the European imperial powers who depended on their African colonies to assist the war effort in human and material contributions.

The period after the Second World War likewise was contradictory for colonial Africa. On the one hand, while Britain and France, as Allied Powers, were victorious, their economies were devastated by the war, their populations were traumatized, and the task of rebuilding was overwhelming. The colonial powers therefore predictably turned to their African colonies for much-needed revenue and raw materials. On the other hand, in the 1950s, reconstruction in Europe having reversed the malaise thanks to the U.S.-financed Marshall Plan, Africa experienced an economic boom. Nevertheless, the reality of colonial rule, its exploitative basis, its failure to provide minimal social services, its denial of what is today known as human rights, was unchanged. Yet, with the emergence of a new superpower, the Soviet Union, which allied itself with the colonized and oppressed peoples of the capitalist world, and with struggles for independence exploding throughout Asia, the colonial powers began to initiate "reforms." For example, although secondary school enrollment in colonial Africa in 1950 was roughly one percent, beginning in the late 1940s new universities were established in a few colonies. Some of these institutions, such as Makerere University in Uganda and University College of the Gold Coast (today the University of Ghana), remain among the premier institutions of higher learning in Africa.

COMPARATIVE COLONIALISM

Within the constraints of the colonial systems, and always bearing in mind the illegality, racist, and predatory nature of colonial rule in general, Africans identified positive and negative aspects of the French and British models. While traditional rulers, like chiefs, possessed a limited degree of power in the British system, for instance, so-called Westernized Africans, those men who were fortunate to acquire Western education, were often looked down upon by colonial officials in the indirect rule system. Colonial administration depended on literate Africans who possessed the necessary skills to function as civil servants, yet they also posed a threat to the colonial state because of their abilities and status as elite Africans. Indeed, as will be shown in chapter 4, these men generally emerged as the leaders of the independence movements throughout Africa. During the early colonial period, however, they were derisively depicted and viewed with suspicion by Europeans. In German Togoland, for example, African men who wore Western clothing and spoke English were dismissed as dandies. In contrast, the development of African elites was encouraged in the French direct rule model in line with its policy of assimilation, and African civil servants could rise much further in that colonial administration than their counterparts in British colonies. Related to this point, the segregation of Africans and Europeans (as well as Asians in the relevant colonies) was characteristic of British rule, particularly in the settler colonies, whereas assimilated Africans in the French system, though they certainly faced discrimination, were not restricted in the same ways.

Another negative consequence of the indirect rule system was that localized identities were fostered and strengthened as the expense of the development of any colonywide political consciousness. Africans voluntarily and involuntarily were grouped into tribes ruled by so-called traditional chiefs, so their sense of belonging to a larger identity, such as Nigerian or Kenyan, was weak or nonexistent at least until the late colonial period. In contrast, the consolidation in the early colonial period of French colonies into super-territories, namely French West Africa with its capital in Dakar and French Equatorial Africa based in Brazzaville, facilitated the eventual formation of Pan African cultural organizations, trade unions, and political parties.

Besides a divergent approach to administration, specifically the role of African chiefs in the colonial bureaucracy, there was a considerable ideological difference between British and French rule. Whereas the British sought to maintain African traditions and customs and keep Africans and Europeans separate, the French promoted the policy of assimilation, which sought to transform Africans into

Frenchmen. Based on the racist notion that assimilation would civilize Africans, the policy nonetheless also promoted an ideal of human equality, albeit limited to those who embraced French language and culture. On a practical level, however, it granted a restricted number of Africans French citizenship as well as representation in the French national assembly in Paris beginning already in 1848 with an elected official from one commune in Senegal extended to four communes in the late 1880s. The determinants for being considered assimilated varied, but most important was proficiency in French, though personal habits related to domestic life, dress, and cultural tastes were important as well.

The theory and practice of assimilation was not limited to French colonial rule. The Portuguese promoted a variation of assimilation in their colonies; called Lusotropicalism, it accepted and to an extent even encouraged sexual relations between European men and African women. There certainly was a significant degree of abuse and exploitation of African women by European men in the Portuguese colonies, but mixed marriages were quite common as well, and the children of such unions, referred to as *mestizos*, often prospered in adulthood by holding important administrative and commercial positions. Indeed, the existence of this so-called mixed-race population was well-established in Portugal's coastal enclaves in Angola and Mozambique in the precolonial period. By the colonial period, the populations of Portuguese colonies were divided into the following hierarchy, from top to bottom: Europeans, *mestizos* and *assimilados* (or assimilated Africans), and *indígenas* (or natives, meaning the majority of Africans).

These cultural distinctions in colonial rule leads prominent Kenyan scholar Ali A. Mazrui to identify two different kinds of racism, which he labels Germanic and Latin. Germanic racism (associated with the British, Germans, Flemish Belgians, and Afrikaners) was race- or blood-based, whereas the Latin form (French, Portuguese, Italians, and Spanish) was rooted in cultural superiority. To explain Mazrui's thesis, we will again focus on British and French colonial rule. Although the French thought they were culturally superior to Africans, as previously noted they believed that Africans could assimilate into French culture. This also means that the mixing of Europeans and Africans was allowed, as evidenced by colonial schools that were not segregated by race. On the other hand, the British strictly segregated Europeans and Africans, frowned on African elites who embraced Western culture, and generally promoted what they considered traditional African culture. Mazrui's discussion of these two types of racism is especially instructive for understanding colonial language policies (and their ramifications on present-day Africa). Whereas the French insisted on the use of their language by all Africans, the British encouraged the use of African languages in administration and education. Some may argue that one sort of racism was less damaging than the other, but Mazrui succinctly observes that "different forms of imperial arrogance had different implications" (Mazrui, *Power of Babel*, 14). Arguably the worst consequences were for those Africans who lived in what are known as the settler colonies, territories in which a tiny minority of European settlers received preferential treatment from the colonial state to the detriment of the majority African population.

SETTLER COLONIES

The settler colonies were grouped in two clusters, one in the far north of Africa, where the most significant European population resided in the French colony of Algeria, and the other in eastern and southern Africa. Rhodesia in 1923 and South Africa in 1931 were granted self-governing status by the British, meaning the European minorities in each (5 and 15 percent, respectively) ruled the majority African populations in strictly segregated and unequal societies. In the major British-ruled settler colonies of Northern Rhodesia and Kenya, the European populations numbered less than one percent. Europeans were encouraged to settle in African colonies with more temperate climates and cash crop potential with such incentives as low-interest loans and free ninety-nine-year leases. The administration of settler colonies presented European colonial officials with special challenges. While European settlers were considered natural allies of the colonial state, they demanded costly social services and economic subsidies, straining the resources of the administration. Settlers were rewarded with the most fertile land, and railways and roads were specially constructed to link settler communities to cities and ports, but they relied on African farmers to cultivate their farms. The dilemma of securing sufficient labor for European settlers was partly solved through the establishment of so-called Native Reserves, but these places also created numerous problems for the colonial administration. Africans were relegated to marginal, impoverished areas of a colony, where the difficulty of practicing agriculture was compounded by overcrowding.

Young men from the reserves thus migrated to European settler farms or urban centers for work while women, children, and the elderly struggled to eke out a living in the reserves.

These conditions often led to the outbreak of diseases, sometimes in areas that were not affected in precolonial times, devastating both human and animal populations. A well-researched case occurred in the eastern part of Northern Rhodesia, where a triad of British colonial officials, the British South Africa Company, and European settlers pursued policies that worsened the living conditions of Africans and even altered the local ecology in the interwar period. European colonial officials seized the most arable land for European settlers, prohibited hunting, and forced Africans into reserves where conditions were deplorable. Many areas set aside for European settlement and farming reverted to bush while the African reserves were wrecked by overuse. As a result, the ecological balance of the area was affected, leading to the spread of the tsetse fly and the resultant outbreak of human and cattle trypanosomiasis (sleeping sickness). Ironically, British colonial officials resorted to traditional African methods of dealing with the tsetse problem, namely, clearing bush and culling wild animals (Vail, "Ecology and History").

Historians have argued that in some ways colonial administrations, rather than acting simply as protectors and promoters of European settlers, were forced to balance competing interests and constituencies, including the settlers, African farmers, and private European commercial enterprises. In fact, these scholars maintain that colonial officials were concerned primarily with guaranteeing social stability, particularly in African communities, even if their motives were not sincere, that is, simply to avoid opposition to colonial rule. Indeed, in some cases colonial officials sought to reign in abusive European settlers and companies when their actions adversely affected African communities. At the same time, the colonial state wanted to strictly enforce segregation, a policy that was fully supported and demanded by European settlers despite the fact they depended on African labor to survive.

Segregation of the races was a key feature of British settler colonies, particularly in urban centers where Africans were confined to what were called African locations. These parts of the cities, sometimes called townships, often emerged as satellites to established cities and were populated by rural migrants. The locations generally lacked basic infrastructure (like sanitation systems), were overcrowded, and congested with inadequate housing. Although it was nominally independent of British rule, South Africa epitomized the severity, difficulties, and contradictions of settler society. As the most urbanized, industrialized, and capitalistic territory in Africa, even in the early colonial period, the European population, largely Afrikaner and thus resident in South Africa for several hundred years, devised a complex system of laws and regulations to control African labor and dispossess Africans of their land. The Native Lands Act of 1913 drastically restricted African property ownership while laws requiring Africans to carry passes had already been enacted.

It is not a coincidence that as the most economically developed and strictly segregated European-ruled territory in Africa, South Africa also was the last to win its independence. When the Afrikaner-dominated National Party came to power in 1948, it implemented step by step the rigid system of apartheid (Afrikaans for separateness) and clamped down on all political activity by Africans. After decades of nonviolent campaigns, in 1960 the African National Congress was banned, and seeing no alternative means of resistance, the organization created an armed military wing called Umkhonto we Sizwe (Spear of the Nation) to fight against apartheid. In many other colonies across the continent, Africans had to resort to violence to win their freedom, a fitting end to a system established through violent conquest, occupation, and suppression.

REFERENCES

District Officers, Intermediaries, and Missionaries
Khapoya, Vincent B. *The African Experience: An Introduction*, Third Edition (New York: Longman, 2010).

Models of Colonial Rule
Crowder, Michael. "Indirect Rule: French and British Style." *Africa: Journal of the International African Institute* 34, no. 3 (1964): 197–205.

Identity and Politics
Ochunu, Moses E. *Colonial Meltdown: Northern Nigeria in the Great Depression* (Athens: Ohio University Press, 2009).

Thomas, Lynn M. *Politics of the Womb: Women, Reproduction, and the State in Kenya* (Berkeley: University of California Press, 2003).

Thuku, Harry. *An Autobiography* (Nairobi: Oxford University Press, 1970).

White, Luise. *Speaking with Vampires: Rumor and History in Colonial Africa* (Berkeley: University of California Press, 2000).

Comparative Colonialism
Mazrui, Ali A. and Alamin M .Mazrui. *The Power of Babel: Language and Governance in the African Experience* (Oxford: James Currey, 1998).

Settler Colonies
Vail, Leroy. "Ecology and History: The Example of Eastern Zambia." *Journal of Southern African Studies* 3, no. 2 (1977): 129–155.

Violence

The violence of European colonialism in Africa, in both its everyday and shocking forms, is often overlooked in popular depictions of the period. Such Hollywood films as the adventure drama *Out of Africa*, with its focus on the relationship between two European settlers in Kenya and its relegation of Africans to the background, bypass the terror and suffering that marked the colonial occupation. Since the colonization of much of the continent occurred suddenly and by agreement and through intimidation and then in many places ended relatively peacefully, the idea that the colonial period was, generally speaking, brutal, bloody, and painful can be forgotten. Likewise, the violence of colonialism did not reach everyone, everywhere, all the time. In Camara Laye's semiautobiographical novel *The Dark Child*, set mostly in a rural community in French-occupied Guinea, the alien influences are subtle, the colonial state is barely present, and rarely is there any mention of Europeans. This was the experience of the narrator and countless other Africans. Nevertheless, in many parts of Africa and for most of the colonial epoch, the colonial experience was characterized by various types of violence. Indeed, violence was such an integral part of European colonial rule in Africa that the subject warrants a closer study.

This chapter examines the subject of violence by dividing up the colonial era into the following periods: first, the early European conquest and occupation of Africa, in which many Africans themselves

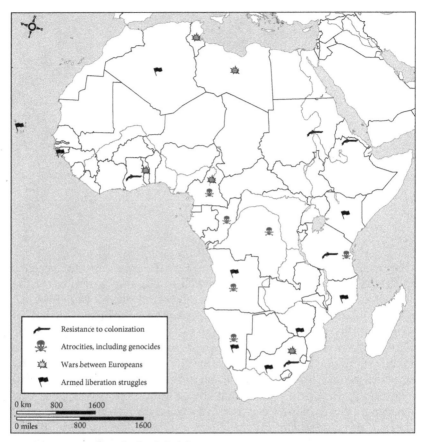

MAP 3   Examples of colonial violence.

took part as hired mercenaries, and the armed defense by African peoples and states against colonization; second, following the so-called pacification phase, the period of African uprisings and European atrocities, exemplified by the genocides in German South-West Africa and the Belgian Congo Free State; third, the world wars, initiated and fought primarily by the European imperial powers but involving millions of African soldiers and playing out on battlefields on the African continent; and fourth, the period of national liberation, during which many Africans had to resort to arms to win their independence and Europeans, in their quest to maintain control of places like Algeria, South Africa, and even the Kenya depicted in

Out of Africa, fought back ruthlessly, disregarding any notion of what we now call human rights.

While today we do not doubt that Africans who fought against colonial rule and for their freedom certainly had the right to self-determination and even the moral high ground against their European colonizers, and though we recognize Africans like Ghana's Kwame Nkrumah and South Africa's Nelson Mandela as visionary heroes, it is important to point out that, for the most part, European imperialists viewed those fighting for their independence with disdain. Familiar terms like "terrorist" were used by the British press, for example, to describe the Kenyans who belonged to the Land and Freedom Party, also derisively known as the Mau Mau, which fought in the 1950s against British rule, and as recently as the early 1990s Mandela was on a list of so-called terrorists maintained by the U.S. government. This rhetoric partly was a reflection of the politics of the Cold War, beginning after the Second World War and lasting until the late 1980s, when the world largely was divided into two, opposed blocs, one headed by the United States, the other by the Soviet Union. The latter, along with other communist nations like China and Cuba, supported the anticolonial movements in Africa to varying degrees, while the United States was allied with those European countries that maintained colonies in Africa as well as the white minority regimes in Rhodesia and South Africa.

These points are raised to emphasize the complexity, contradictions, and consistencies of history. The common phrase "one person's freedom fighter is another person's terrorist" is applicable to sentiments expressed in the late colonial period in Africa. And the same person who was imprisoned and called a terrorist and a communist by a government that purported to defend democracy and capitalism in Africa later became the first democratically elected president of that country and a man celebrated worldwide for his strength and character. That person, of course, is Mandela and the country is South Africa, the last nation in Africa to achieve its independence from European rule. But, the fight against colonial occupation began at its inception, as African armies tried to defend their territories against far better equipped, European-led forces.

CONQUEST AND RESISTANCE

In 1898, the British poet Hilaire Belloc penned the well-known verse: "Whatever happens we have got/The maxim-gun and they have not"

("The Modern Traveller"). These simple lines neatly summarize the early period of conquest and resistance. Whatever deliberations occurred among Africans on the issue of signing treaties with Europeans, regardless of the decisions they ultimately made, and no matter if their armies fought against occupation, Europeans possessed overwhelming military superiority in the battlefield. While most African soldiers were armed with early-nineteenth-century muskets, which took at least a minute to load and quite often misfired, European armies were furnished with the latest weaponry, including the aforementioned Maxim machine gun that fired eleven bullets per second. The devastation wrecked by this new weapon was epitomized by the Battle of Omdurman, which took place in the same year that Belloc wrote those words in what today is the outskirts of Sudan's capital, Khartoum. A vastly larger army, perhaps numbering fifty thousand, commanded by Abdullah al-Taashi, leader of the Sudanese Madhist state, was slaughtered by a combined force of British, Sudanese, and Egyptians led by the British general Herbert Kitchener. The Madhist soldiers charged the British lines repeatedly and were plowed down by the machine guns wielded by the British troops. At the end of the battle, nearly eleven thousand Madhists were dead, whereas a mere forty-nine British soldiers had lost their lives. This lopsided death toll was not unique to the battle at Omdurman but was repeated across the continent as even the most disciplined, well-organized, and battle-hardened armies, including those of Asante in West Africa and the Zulu in southern Africa, were defeated by British colonial forces. It should be pointed out, however, that there were African victories, too, most famously at the Battle of Adwa (1896), where the Ethiopian army of Emperor Menelik decisively defeated Italian forces invading from Eritrea on the Red Sea coast.

Yet, as revealed by Omdurman, Europeans did not fight their battles alone but rather, relied on African recruits, perhaps more accurately termed mercenaries, to defeat African armies. The French had been employing African fighters since the 1850s, attracting many slaves and ex-slaves to a colonial army corps known as the Tirailleurs Sénégalais (French for Senegalese skirmishers or sharp-shooters) created in 1857. Despite the name, they eventually were recruited from throughout what became the French African empire and in addition to fighting alongside French soldiers in conquering the West African savannah were employed in French Equatorial Africa, Algeria, Morocco, Madagascar and beyond during the two world wars. Although the French were first to organize such a force, other colonial powers also relied on African soldiers in their colonial wars. The colonial army in German East Africa, for example, was composed mostly of so-called *askaris*, African soldiers recruited from particular ethnic groups in the colony as well as faraway Sudan. Relatively well-paid, highly trained and disciplined, the *askaris* were instrumental in suppressing resistance to German rule as well as in defending the colony against Allied invasion during the First World War. The British equivalent was the King's African Rifles, a regiment that was similar in composition to the German forces and also was deployed primarily in East Africa, until the group was disbanded in 1960.

In addition to the mainly African composition of the European armies, the colonial wars were further complicated by mixed allegiances and unanticipated outcomes. The South Africa War (formerly known as the Boer War) illustrates this point. The conflict of 1899–1902 principally was between the British who dominated southern Africa and were extending their colonial occupation northward and the Afrikaners (the so-called Boers), mainly farmers of mixed-European background who also were expanding their settlements and thus coming into conflict with African peoples and states. The Afrikaners formed alliances with Africans who opposed British colonization, the British enjoyed the support of Africans who lost their land to Afrikaner settlement or suffered the brutality of slave-like conditions on their farms, while still other Africans did not involve themselves in what they regarded as a conflict between European imperialists. In any event, Africans fought on both sides of the war, which resulted in the largest loss of life for the British in Africa and was notorious for the British use of internment camps. Africans suffered huge casualities in the conflict, in which they ultimately were the biggest losers.

The consequences of European victories and African defeats were not limited to the loss of life and independence but had other far-reaching and destructive ramifications, such as famines and the spread of diseases. Many parts of the continent were devastated by conquest and by the turn of the century, Europeans declared pacification a success. Nevertheless, many areas of their colonies remained outside their authority, and even some of those places that were supposedly pacified rose up in rebellion in the early 1900s. European colonial regimes suppressed those uprisings with brutal force and often used the same tactics to impose their economic demands. As the following cases make clear, the latter often preceded the rebellions.

UPRISINGS AND ATROCITIES

The first genocide of the twentieth century did not take place in Europe or Asia; it was carried out by the Germans against the Herero in the German South-West Africa colony (present-day Namibia) from 1904 to 1907 in what the historical literature calls the Herero uprising. The Herero's pastoralist economy had been increasingly threatened by German colonial policies since the late 1880s. First, the German colonial regime encouraged European settlement and expropriated African land for European settler farms. Then, it laid railways through Herero territory, cutting off pastures for their cattle, and resettled many Herero on reserves created with the support of European missionaries. Following the 1897 outbreak of rinderpest, an infectious viral disease that killed most of the Herero's cattle herds, colonial abuses multiplied as agents peddled grossly exploitative loans in exchange for land, German officials and settlers arbitrarily and cruelly punished and imprisoned Herero men for so-called offenses, and the rape of Herero women and girls was widespread.

The Herero decided that nearly two decades of colonial exploitation and violence were enough, and under the command of paramount chief Samuel Maherero, they declared war against the German colonists in January 1904. Their goal was straightforward, namely, to win back their land, and Maherero issued specific instructions to his soldiers, most remarkably that European women and children as well as missionaries should not be harmed, and he forewarned the German colonial regime about his intent to fight. In a letter to the German governor, Maherero declared:

> The outbreak of this war was not initiated by me in this year, rather it was begun by the whites. How many Hereros have the whites, particularly the traders, killed? Both by guns and by locking them up in the prisons. And each time I have brought these cases to Windhoek [the colony's capital] the blood of my people always had to pay. ... Many of the traders have exacerbated the difficulties by shifting their debts onto my people. And when something like this occurred you shot us. ... These things have led to the outbreak of war in this country. (Gewald, *Herero Heroes*, 167)

The German response to the uprising was carefully planned, comprehensive, and vicious. In order to recruit volunteers in Europe, the uprising was described as a race war with the Herero depicted as brutal savages intent on killing Europeans. Lt. Gen. Lothar von Trotha, a German commander with experience smashing resistance to colonial rule in German East Africa (present-day Tanzania), was directed to lead the ten-thousand-strong army of European mercenaries assembled to annihilate the Herero. The Vernichtungsbefehl (destruction order) he issued was chillingly clear: "Within the German borders, every Herero, whether armed or unarmed, shall be shot."

The genocide was carried out through various means, but perhaps the most atrocious was what one German officer called a "march into death." German soldiers forced Herero families into the Omaheke desert, sealed the perimeter with guard towers, then poisoned the wells. The emancipated Herero who attempted to escape starvation were bayoneted by waiting European soldiers, while others faced a slow, painful death in the desert. An official history produced by the German general staff later concluded: "The arid Omaheke was to complete what the German army had begun: the annihilation of the Herero people."

It has been estimated that more than eighty percent of the Herero died during the genocide, either directly murdered by the Germans or indirectly through starvation and disease. The survivors were rounded up and locked up in concentration camps, where the Germans grouped captured Herero soldiers along with women and children, all of whom were punished with forced labor. Clearly, there are many parallels with the Holocaust carried out by Nazi Germany about three decades later—namely, the initial destruction order, concentration camps, and civilians forced into labor. In fact, Adolf Hitler was influenced by the so-called scientific research carried out on "race-mixing" by German geneticist Eugen Fischer in German-ruled South-West Africa. His conclusion, that mixed-race children are mentally and physically inferior to the offspring of German parents, was cited in Hitler's manifesto *Mein Kampf.*

Around the same time, genocide took place to the north in the Congo Free State, a personal possession awarded to Belgian king Leopold II at the Berlin Conference. This enormous territory, comprising the vast Congo basin at the center of the African continent and known today as the Democratic Republic of Congo, was run as a corporation headed by Leopold named the Association internationale africaine from 1885 to 1908. Virtually the entire population of the territory was conscripted in the collection of wild rubber, with unrealistic quotas mandated and an armed forced called the Force Publique established to enforce them. Comprised of Belgian officers and African soldiers and armed with the hated *chicotte* (a whip made of hippo skin), the force not only beat, tortured, and raped Africans but also chopped off the limbs of men, women, and children as punishment for not meeting the rubber quota. A famous photo from the time shows an African man staring blankly at the severed hand and foot of his five-year-old daughter lying on the ground while written reports of the time describe Belgian district officers proudly producing baskets of hands and feet to their superiors as evidence of their implementation of policy.

The violence of Leopold's rubber terror devastated whole regions of the colony, as villages were burned, men were forced into rubber collection and other activities, women and children were kidnapped to be held as hostages, and normal economic and social activities ground to a halt. Scholarly estimates of the deaths range from twenty to fifty percent of the population of the Congo Free State, or ten million people, as a result of famine, outbreak of diseases, and depopulation. The mayhem ended only after firsthand accounts by journalists and missionaries, as well as Joseph Conrad's novel *The Heart of Darkness*, based on his personal experiences in the colony, led to an international humanitarian campaign to end the atrocities. As the Belgian parliament annexed the Congo Free State in 1908, and thus disposed the king of his personal colony, Leopold ordered all documents from his reign to be burned, purportedly declaring: "They can have my Congo, but they will never know what I did there!" The conditions in Congo were most widely publicized, but forced and brutal rubber campaigns also were carried out in the neighboring colonies of French Congo, German Cameroon, and Portuguese Angola.

Although the term *genocide* has not been used to describe other cases of mass killings by Europeans during the colonial period, German South-West Africa and the Congo Free State were not the only colonies where these kinds of atrocities occurred. Another well-known uprising, called the Maji Maji Rebellion that occurred between 1905 and 1907 in German East Africa, had similar causes and outcomes. Peasants who were overwhelmed by German demands for unpaid labor on cotton fields, among other abuses, rose up against the colonial regime, protected by what they believed to be water medicine (*maji*) that would repel bullets. Colonial forces, comprising mostly African *askaris* commanded by Germans, crushed the rebellion. Depopulation and famine occurred as a result of the destruction of villages and crops, causing up to two hundred thousand deaths.

By the First World War, the era of uprisings, usually ethnically based, localized, and led by traditional rulers, for lack of a better term, came to an end. Just as the imperial powers declared war against one another, and the colonial map of Africa was amended one last time following Germany's defeat, the colonial regimes could claim they had control over the entire continent with the exceptions of Liberia and Ethiopia. The era of world wars, however, not only ushered in new strategies, alliances, and leadership in the resistance to colonial rule, but it also witnessed the large-scale deployment of African soldiers to fight Europe's battles.

WORLD WARS

The horrors of the world wars are familiar to many readers: the use of mustard gas and horrendous trench warfare of the First World War and the crematoriums, fire bombing, and atomic weaponry of the Second World War. But less well known is the role African soldiers played in these largely European conflicts, as hundreds of thousands of African men traveled thousands of miles from their homes to fight in distant combat zones. Moreover, key battles in both wars were fought on African soil, and Europeans relied on their colonies for material aid for their military campaigns worldwide.

The First World War of 1914–1918, also known as the Great War, was essentially between the European imperial powers, which nonetheless depended on Africa for material and human resources throughout the conflict. The war's impact on Africa was significant: besides the African men who fought and lost their lives in battles or were forced into war-related labor, Europeans extracted raw materials and cash crops at an unprecedented scale to raise revenues and supply and feed their armies. Of the roughly two hundred thousand West Africans who fought in the First World War, 192,000 were members of the Tirailleurs Sénégalais, which drew recruits from throughout French Africa but mostly West Africa. In the decades preceding the conflict, the corps had been built up to provide a standing colonial army for France in Africa. Impressed by their performance in the conquest period and guided by racist thinking that West Africans were natural soldiers, the French relied on the Tirailleurs Sénégalais to quell rebellions and defend positions throughout their colonies. While some volunteered to join the Tirailleurs Sénégalais, responding to colonial appeals that promised retirement benefits, the majority who fought in the First World War were conscripted into service. In addition to participating in campaigns in

Turkey and the German colonies of Togoland and Cameroon, Tirailleurs Sénégalais soliders fought in Europe, where they confronted special challenges. So many fell victim to frostbite on the infamous Western Front that the French army would relocate them to southern France during the winter. When a small number served as part of the Allied forces occupying the Rhineland in Germany after the war, West African soliders faced racist discrimination. In addition to suffering the high mortality rates in battle associated with the First World War, many African soldiers perished as a result of diseases, such as tuberculosis. Some thirty thousand West Africans died in the First World War.

For his study on the Tirailleurs Sénégalais, historian Joe Lunn collected the accounts of Senegalese veterans of the First World War, offering readers firsthand accounts of their time in the colonial army. Reading the interview excerpts Lunn incorporates into his book, it is apparent that these men have mixed emotions about their wartime experience, sharing the horrors and pain of war and racism but also the pride of fighting bravely. One veteran, Masserigne Somare, recounts what transpired after a combat victory:

> We felt very proud after the attack because the French had tried many times to retake the fort, but finally, we [were the ones] who took it. ... And when we were leaving the fort, our officers told us not to wash our uniforms even though they were very dirty and covered with mud. But we were told: "Don't wash your uniforms. Cross the country as you are so that everyone who meets you will know that you made the attack on Fort Douaumont." And we took the train [and traveled] for three days between Douaumont and St. Raphäel. And in every town we crossed, the French were clapping their hands and shouting: "Vive les tirailleurs sénégalais!" (*Memoirs of the Maelstrom*, 137).

According to the veterans, this pride and their general wartime experiences translated into a newfound confidence that they took home with them to Senegal and posed a challenge to the European colonial order. One veteran's son, Aliou Dioama, recalls of his father:

> When [my father] came back, he had learned many things from the war and [about] the "white" man. ... He had gained more understanding about the kinds of ways officials should [behave]. So he contributed a lot to the change of many things. Because he said "no" when he was [within his rights] to say "no" and "yes" [only] when he [decided] to say "yes." And he didn't accept any longer this official cheating [of] people or telling [them] something that was not true (192).

A veteran, Ibrahima Thiam, addresses the same topic:

> The war changed many, many things. At first, when we joined the army, when you had an argument or a problem with a "white" man, what happened? You were wrong; you were [always] wrong. But later, those things changed. [Then] they looked into the matter and determined who was wrong or right. [But] before that time, the "black" man didn't mean anything. So that [change] was something [very important]. [And] the respect we gained [from] the war [continued] increasing; it never [diminished]. [And this] respect [continued] increasing day to day—up until [it culminated in] the Independence Day. (233)

Nevertheless, these soldiers quickly were reminded that they lived in a colonial state in which severe restrictions were placed on the economic, political, and social life of Africans. As another veteran, Sera Ndiaye, recalls more critically: "We went to France, we fought for France, and the French took us by force to fight for them. [But] we learned nothing [there]—[not] even the French language. They only taught us some rudimentary [commands], [in order] to use us in the war" (230).

African soldiers had similar experiences in the Second World War, an even more destructive and devastating conflict that the first. Almost two million Africans were drafted into the European armies during the war, nearly four hundred thousand serving in the British army by the end of the war in 1945. The Tirailleurs Sénégalais once more played a crucial role, this time helping to liberate France from German occupation. Additionally, some of the most important battles between the Axis and Allied powers took place in North Africa, particularly Libya and Tunisia, and involved African soldiers from across the continent. The experience of war again had unintended consequences, from the perspective of the European colonialists. Fighting side by side, African soldiers saw Europeans in a very different light from the one back home. While colonial officials and other Europeans sought to project themselves as superior to Africans, on the battlefield Africans recognized their European counterparts as physical, emotional, and intellectual equals. Furthermore, the hypocrisy of defending the freedom and independence of England and France when Africans themselves were colonized was too obvious. Why should they risk their lives for the defense of their colonial masters when they were not free themselves? The Senegalese writer and director Ousmane Sembène, considered to be the father of African cinema, was conscripted into the French army. He served as a truck driver and later a chauffeur in Charles de Gaulle's Free French forces. Like countless other African men, the wartime experience, particularly ordinary daily interactions, shaped Sembène's anticolonial politics. He later recalled, "In the army we saw those who considered themselves our masters naked, in tears, some cowardly or ignorant ... when a white soldier asked me to write a letter for him, it was a revelation—I thought Europeans knew how to write. The war demystified the colonizer; the veil fell" (*Independent*, 13 June 2007). Indeed, African soldiers returned home from the Second World War deeply politicized and at the forefront of a new generation of resistance to colonial rule.

Humbled and economically ruined by the war, Britain and France were now faced with demands for self-rule, not reforms of the colonial system, and though they tried to postpone and direct the transition from colonial rule to independence, in the late 1950s and early 1960s they generally gave up and retreated from Africa. In most cases, independence was won through nonviolent means, in the form of protests, boycotts, and petitions, but in a few places, specifically settler colonies, Africans were forced to resort to arms to win their freedom. As Mandela once observed, "It is the oppressor, not the oppressed, who sets the terms of the struggle."

Despite the winds of changes worldwide, as many colonies in Africa and beyond regained their independence in the era of decolonization, Europeans clung to a few prized colonial possessions, refusing to relinquish control and ready to suppress all anticolonial movements.

ARMED LIBERATION STRUGGLES

The Algerian war for independence, which lasted from 1954 to 1962, was one of the bloodiest anticolonial struggles of the twentieth century. It resulted in the deaths of hundreds of thousands of Algerians and others and was marked by the widespread use of torture and blatant disregard for civilians. It also is one of the best documented conflicts in African history, as countless French officials and soldiers published their personal accounts and, more famously, the horrors of the war were depicted in the cinematic masterpiece *The Battle of Algiers*.

A colonial possession since 1830, the French considered Algeria an integral part of France, an extension of the nation. Not only was the Algerian coastline a short boat trip across the Mediterranean

Young Algerian women with fair complexions could pass as Europeans at French military checkpoints, as depicted in this scene from the 1966 film *Battle of Algiers*. Such women were key activists in the National Liberation Front's extended bombing campaign of European cafés and social centers in Algiers from 1954 to 1960.

from southern France, but hundreds of thousands of European settlers, especially of French, Italian, and Spanish origin, lived there. But, as was the case in colonies throughout Africa, French occupation had terrible consequences for the Algerians, and in 1954 the National Liberation Front, known by the French acronym FLN, declared a war for independence.

Waging a guerrilla war, and supported by its newly independent neighbors Tunisia and Morocco, the FLN persevered against considerable odds. The far better equipped French forces were led by commanders with valuable wartime experience, particularly in the French resistance in the Second World War and, more recently, fighting the anticolonial Viet Minh movement in Vietnam. Moreover, the French successfully isolated and encircled FLN forces, erecting an electrified fence along the Tunisian border and closing off entire neighborhoods in the cities, and embraced torture as a means of extracting information from captured FLN soldiers. In the Algerian conflict, too, the French relied primarily on African soldiers to suppress the anticolonial movement. Known as the *harkis*, the Algerian men who professed loyalty to France and fought against the FLN were targeted by the FLN for their collaboration with the French.

On their side, the FLN was comprised of semiautonomous divisions from across the colony, each fighting the enemy in its own way in urban centers like Algiers and Oran, in interior zones like the Kabyle
· mountains, or far away in the Sahara Desert. In Algiers, the capital, the FLN engaged in what today might be called terrorist acts, as cafés and social centers popular with European settlers were targeted in an extended bombing campaign from 1954 to 1960. Since colonial authorities generally restricted Algerian men, who were always suspected of being FLN members, young Algerian women with fair complexions who might pass as European were recruited and trained to carry out these attacks by casually walking into a settler venue and leaving behind a purse containing a bomb. These attacks succeeded in sowing terror within the European community, but predictably it also brought a backlash as Algerians were indiscriminately assaulted and murdered by settler mobs and the French authorities sealed off and raided house by house the Casbah district of Algiers. The FLN bombing campaign and the French response are dramatically portrayed in *The Battle of Algiers*, which is based on a book by an FLN commander.

The Algerian struggle for independence was unique in a number of ways. Besides the war between the French colonial forces and the FLN, a second conflict emerged as European settlers formed various paramilitary organizations, principally the Organization of the Secret Army (OAS), which carried out terrorist attacks on Algerian civilians and French officials in order to prevent Algerian independence. With a rallying cry of "Algeria is French and will remain so," the OAS was notorious for its indiscriminate use of plastic explosives. Moreover, both conflicts played out in France itself, where the FLN collected funds among the Algerian migrant community to support the war effort in Algeria and carried out targeted assassinations of Algerians with other loyalties, and the European settler groups also executed terrorist attacks against governmental authorities and buildings. In Algeria, settler leaders allied with sympathetic French military officials overthrew the French colonial governor in 1960 and nearly succeeded in assassinating President de Gaulle in 1962. That same year, after almost a decade of war, approximately one million Algerian causalities, protracted negotiations between de Gaulle's government and the FLN, and an overwhelming plebiscite vote in favor of independence, the French relented. In the months leading up to Algerian independence, nearly ten percent of the population, including the vast majority of the European settlers as well as many Algerian *harkis* who fought on the French side, fled Algeria by sea and air, convinced they would not be welcomed in an independent Algeria and fearful of the consequences if they stayed to find out.

Africans in the European settler colony of Kenya also resorted to guerilla warfare to win back their independence after decades of land alienation, forced labor, segregation, and other policies that denied them economic and political rights. As explained in the preceding chapters, European colonial officials barred Africans from growing certain cash crops and sought to restrict them to reserves and locations as a means to ensure a steady supply of cheap labor for European settlers in the so-called White Highlands. Beginning in the early 1940s with such actions as setting fire to the buildings, livestock, and crops on European settler farms, this primarily Kikuyu, rural movement expanded in scope and tactics leading to targeted attacks on European settlers and African chiefs viewed as collaborators. In 1952,

Kenyan suspected of being a participant of the Mau Mau uprising being arrested by British soldiers (date unknown). During the rebellion, hundreds of thousands of African men were sent to concentration camps established by the British, who also employed torture, rape, and summary executions in their campaign to end the insurgency.

British colonial authorities declared a state of emergency, and leaders of the Mau Mau uprising, as it became known for the secret oath that fighters were required to take but was called the Land and Freedom Party by Kenyans themselves, were arrested and imprisoned, including Jomo Kenyatta. The colonial press carried exaggerated and hysterical accounts of the Mau Mau struggle, describing it as a race war, much like German authorities characterized the Herero uprising in the early colonial period. The British, ruthlessly seeking to crush the Mau Mau movement, conducted aerial bombardments of Kikuyu areas, resettled entire communities in isolated and closed villages, and imprisoned terrorists, as they were called, and alleged accomplices in concentration camps.

Our knowledge of the true severity of the British war against the Mau Mau has expanded greatly over the past few years, thanks to the diligent research of academics and human rights activists. Most prominently, historian Caroline Elkins's book *Imperial Reckoning* presents the "untold story" of this tragic episode in African colonial history based on uncovered archival documents and interviews with Mau Mau fighters and survivors of the concentration camps. British colonial officials and their African accomplices in the so-called Home Guard engaged in psychological warfare to break the spirit of communities they suspected of supporting the insurgency. As one woman recalls:

> At one point, all the villagers were ordered to remove every article of clothing and remain stark naked. You cannot start to imagine the shame and embarrassment we felt when, without any consideration for the small children, we were told to arrange ourselves in two rows, one for the men and the other for the women, old and young alike. To everyone's horror we were ordered at gunpoint to embrace each other, man with a woman, regardless if whether that man happened to be your father, your father-in-law, or brother. It was all so humiliating that one woman hanged herself later, as she felt that she could not continue to live with the humiliating experience of having been forced to embrace her son-in-law while both of them were naked. In our custom that is a curse. (249)

Physical torture, rape, and summary executions also were pervasive in the British campaign Another woman remembers:

> We were beaten the whole day until evening, when we were separated from the men, who were ordered to sit a distance away with their hands cuffed together. Then the interrogators started to squeeze their private parts with a pair of pliers.

There was only a short distance between where they were and ourselves. I even saw one of them being hit on his face, a blow that sent him sprawling down unconscious. A whole bucket of water had to be poured on his body to revive him. The same evening, the men were loaded onto a vehicle and driven away. We were to learn the following morning that all of them had been executed. That night all of the women including myself were divided amongst the Home Guards and raped. Even this lady who was eight months pregnant was not spared. We were raped throughout the night. The following morning we were anxious to know the fate of the men. I remember asking the same pregnant woman what happened to our men after they were castrated. She pointed to a vehicle which was a short distance away. The bodies of our men lay inside. They had already been killed. (257)

Retreating to the forests, and despite the fact that hundreds of thousands of men were sent to the concentration camps, the Mau Mau fighters continued the fight against British colonial rule until the insurgency was essentially defeated in 1956. Debate continues on the number of Kenyans who were killed in what British colonial officials called the Emergency, but recent scholarship has put the estimate at twenty thousand lives, though some argue the true figure is much higher. Despite their victory over the Mau Mau, the British were struck by the perseverance and widespread support of the guerrilla fighters, as well as the liability of defending the small community of European settlers, and slowly began preparations for the independence of Kenya that finally came in 1963.

With the exception of French Tunisia and British Northern Rhodesia, Africans in the other European settler colonies also engaged in armed struggle to win their freedom from colonial rule. In Angola and Mozambique (and the nonsettler colonies of Guinea and Cape Verde), Africans took up arms in the 1960s to force out the Portuguese, the first European imperial power in Africa and the last to leave. By then, the global political balance had changed considerably, as the Cold War between the United States and the Soviet Union introduced a new dimension to the anticolonial struggle in Africa and beyond. The United States was allied with Africa's colonial masters, including Portugal, and many Africans believed that the Americans certainly did not have the moral authority to criticize colonial rule since it too possessed colonies like Puerto Rico where it also suppressed an independence movement. In addition, the American civil rights struggle, with which Africans naturally sympathized and identified, revealed the hypocrisy of American rhetoric championing freedom and democracy in opposition to Soviet communism as African

Americans and other minorities fought against segregation and other forms of inequality. For their part, the Soviets presented themselves as supporters and defenders of colonized peoples worldwide and provided military, humanitarian, and moral support to those fighting colonial rule in places like Vietnam. This assistance was extended, albeit sparingly and cautiously at first, to Africans fighting for independence from the Portuguese, European settlers in Rhodesia, and the white minority in apartheid South Africa.

Independence came first for the Portuguese settler colonies in 1974, when a left-wing military coup ousted the fascist dictatorship in Lisbon and quickly granted independence to all of Portugal's African colonies, both out of ideological sympathy for the anticolonial struggle and from exhaustion over the human and material costs of clinging to their colonies despite the winds of change worldwide. Rhodesia was next, where, after decades of guerrilla warfare by two African armies, one backed by the Soviet Union and the other by China, the white minority regime was finally convinced to give up. Africans declared independence in 1980 and renamed their county Zimbabwe after the ancient Shona empire. The armed struggle continued into the late 1980s in South-West Africa and South Africa, however, and epitomized the conflict between the two superpowers, as the United States cautioned against a communist takeover of capitalist South Africa and the Soviet Union and its allies, particularly Cuba, provided a remarkable degree of support to the antiapartheid movement, as we will be shown in the next chapter. In spite of this discussion of the armed struggles for independence, in the vast majority of colonies Africans achieved their independence without having to take up arms. In fact, the transition from colonial rule to independence was a relatively peaceful, deliberate, and collegial negotiation between European colonial rulers and the leaders of Africa's independence movements.

REFERENCES

Laye, Camara. *The Dark Child* (New York: Farrar, Straus and Giroux, 1954).

Uprisings and Atrocities
Gewald, Jan-Bart. Herero Heroes: *A Socio-Political History of the Herero on Namibia, 1890–1923* (Oxford: James Currey, 1999).

Hochschild, Adam. *King Leopold's Ghost: A Story of Greed, Terror, and Heroism in Colonial Africa* (Boston: Houghton Mifflin, 1999).

World Wars
Lunn, Joe. *Memoirs of the Maelstrom: A Senegalese Oral History of the First World War* (Portsmouth, U.K.: Heinemann, 1999).

Armed Liberation Struggles
Elkins, Caroline. *Imperial Reckoning: The Untold Story of Britain's Gulag in Kenya* (New York: Henry Holt, 2005).

Horne, Alistair. *A Savage War of Peace: Algeria 1954–1962* (New York: New York Review of Books, 1977).

Shubin, V. G. *The "Hot" Cold War: The USSR in Southern Africa* (London: Pluto, 2008).

Liberation

Addressing a massive, rapturous crowd in the early morning hours of March 6, 1957, the date of the Gold Coast colony's independence from Britain, Kwame Nkrumah, the first president of the new nation of Ghana, named after an ancient empire in honor of Africa's precolonial history, declared:

> At long last, the battle has ended! And thus Ghana, your beloved country is free forever. And yet again I want to take the opportunity to thank the chiefs and people of this country, the youth, the farmers, the women who have so nobly fought and won this battle. Also I want to thank the valiant ex-service men who have so co-operated with me in this mighty task of freeing our country from foreign rule and imperialism. ...
>
> I made it quite clear that from now on—today—we must change our attitudes, our minds, we must realise that from now on, we are no more a colonial but a free and independent people. But also, as I pointed out, that also entails hard work. That new African is ready to fight his own battles and show that after all, the black man is capable of managing his own affairs. We are going to demonstrate to the world, to the other nations, that we are prepared to lay our own foundation. As I said in the assembly just minutes ago, I made a point that we are going to create our own African personality and identity. It is the only way that we can show the world that we are ready for our own battles. ...
>
> Our independence is meaningless unless it is linked up with the total liberation of Africa. Let us now fellow Ghanaians, let us now ask for God's blessing and

for only two seconds in your thousands and millions, I want to ask you to pause only for one minute and give thanks to almighty God for having led us through our difficulties, imprisonments, hardships and suffering to have brought us to the end of our troubles today. ...

I am depending upon the millions of the country, and the chiefs and people, to help me to reshape the destiny of this country. We are prepared to pick it up and make it a nation that will be respected by every nation in the world. We know we are going to have difficult beginnings, but again, I'm relying upon your support, I'm relying upon your hard work. Seeing you in this ... it doesn't matter how far my eye goes, I can see that you are here in your millions and my last warning to you is that you are to stand firm behind us so that we can prove to the world that when the African is given a chance he can show the world that he is somebody! We have awakened. We will not sleep anymore. Today, from now on, there is a new African in the world!

This excerpt from what is popularly known as the "Midnight Speech" neatly summarizes the fight against European colonial rule and the challenges facing newly independent African countries. The victory over colonialism, even in those colonies where Africans did not have to resort to violence, was a hard and difficult struggle, during which countless people were imprisoned and otherwise persecuted, one that was fought by ordinary men and women, such as farmers, traders, and veterans, but led by Western-educated elites like Nkrumah. The anticolonial movement was sparked not only by the injustices that Africans faced under European colonial rule and the natural desire of all humans for freedom from oppression but also by the inspiration of ideas and struggles from beyond, particularly the shared experiences of African peoples worldwide. At a time when Africans around the world faced racism, segregation, and colonial rule, particularly on the African continent, Nkrumah and other Africans were determined to disprove those who doubted the ability of Africans to govern themselves, then a prevailing European sentiment, and to assist other Africans who remained under colonial rule, such as those in the European settler colonies of southern Africa.

This chapter examines the African struggle for independence from European colonial rule, especially the ideologies that influenced anticolonial organizations. Each of the movements for independence across Africa were shaped by local conditions, such as the specific grievances against the colonial regime; relations between ethnic

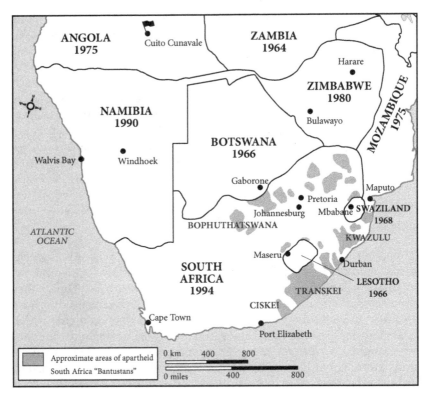

MAP 4 Liberation in southern Africa

groups, classes, and the sexes; and the particular experiences of colonial rule. In some colonies, independence was achieved by relatively peaceful, negotiated means, whereas in others, freedom from colonial rule came only after protracted, violent conflict. Nevertheless, we can identify a number of transnational ideologies that not only influenced the specific demands of independence struggles but also guided their rhetoric and organization. Chief among these were Pan-Africanism and Marxism and, for parts of the continent, Islam and Christianity.

PAN-AFRICANISM

The first batch of colonies to win their independence was in North Africa, starting with Egypt in 1922 (though the British maintained a military presence there until 1947). With the exception of Algeria (discussed in chapter 3), the remaining North African colonies became independent in the following decade: Libya in 1951 and Morocco, Tunisia, as well as Sudan in 1956. A variety of ideologies—nationalist, communist, Islamic—influenced the independence movements in North Africa, where the earliest parties associated with each, such as Tunisia's nationalist Destour Party, Egypt's Communist Party, and the Muslim Brotherhood of Egypt, played key roles in the struggle against colonial rule. The first colony in sub-Saharan African to win its independence was Ghana in 1957, and its example, and especially the rhetoric of its president Nkrumah, inspired other anticolonial movements throughout the continent.

Indeed, Nkrumah emerged as the leader of a new, more militant generation of Pan-Africanists. The roots of Pan-Africanism stretch back to the nineteenth century, when a number of Western-educated West Africans formulated the idea of Ethiopianism, derived from the biblical verse "Ethiopia shall soon stretch out her hands unto God." Often frustrated by the discrimination they personally faced dealing with Europeans, and generally in opposition to the prevailing ideology of racism of the time, they sought to defend African culture in light of the scorn and condemnation by European Christian missionaries in West Africa. This influence was most evident in the establishment of independent African churches, beginning in the 1860s, and took hold especially in South Africa, where it most fully developed into an ideology of resistance against alien rule. Concurrent with Ethiopianism was the concept of an "African Personality," first articulated by academic and politician Edward Blyden. Born on the Caribbean island of St. Thomas but living most of his life in Liberia, Blyden employed the language of the time to argue that Africans constituted a "Great Race," and the legacy of his ideas is evident in the words of Nkrumah which began this chapter.

In the early twentieth century, the key figures in the Pan-Africanist movement were Marcus Garvey and W. E. B. Du Bois. Garvey was a Jamaican who worked and studied in various parts of the Atlantic world, including Central America and Britain, where he was struck by the common experiences of black peoples, namely, discrimination and oppression. Influenced by the writings of an earlier generation of Pan-Africanists, as well as the African American leader Booker T. Washington, Garvey first founded the Universal Negro Improvement Society (UNIA) in 1914 in Jamaica and then in 1918 in the United States the influential newspaper *Negro World*. Based in New York, Garvey attracted a wide following, advocating a return to

Africa for those in diaspora, the establishment of black-owned businesses, and generally promoting pride in African identity, history, and culture. At its height, UNIA had millions of members and chapters throughout Africa and the diaspora as well as a shipping business called the Black Star line, which was intended to ferry Africans in the diaspora back to the continent. Although scholars debate the success of Garvey's schemes and criticize what some consider to be flamboyant aspects of his personality, such as his penchant for presenting himself as a monarch, his influence in colonial Africa was widespread. UNIA organizers traveled to West and South Africa, distributing *Negro World* (which was banned by colonial authorities), and establishing local chapters throughout both regions of the continent. Indeed, historians have discovered reports by European colonial officials raising concerns about Garveyism as rumors about the coming of a black king to liberate Africa spread in rural communities. Many of the first generation of African leaders, including Nkrumah and Kenyatta, as well as early anticolonial figures like Harry Thuku (discussed in chapter 2), were strongly influenced by Garveyism.

The other towering figure of early twentieth century Pan-Africanism was Du Bois, the African American intellectual and activist who penned such groundbreaking books as *The Souls of Black Folk*. A founder of the early civil rights group the National Association for the Advancement of Colored People and toward the end of his life a member of the American Communist Party, Du Bois also advocated pride in African identity but tied the struggle of blacks with those of other colonized and oppressed peoples around the world. In other words, as a Marxist thinker, Du Bois saw capitalism as the cause of oppression, not the escape from it as Garvey argued. Du Bois understood segregation and colonialism as inherent in capitalism—after all, according to Lenin, imperialism is the highest stage of capitalism—and thus viewed the struggle against colonial rule in Africa and segregation in the United States and oppression globally as a fight against capitalism, one that would be won only with the transformation to socialism. Du Bois was not alone among major Pan-Africanist figures of the time for his radical political ideas, and as a result of a series of Pan-Africanist congresses that were held over several decades, beginning with the first in Paris in 1919, he became recognized as the leader of the movement. At these meetings, which were held outside of Africa, often in the capitals of European imperial powers, Africans from throughout the continent and across the diaspora met to discuss the plight of black people and to generate petitions demanding the end of the abuses of colonial rule and segregation. The most influential and largest of these congresses took place under the leadership of Du Bois in 1945 in Manchester, England, where many recently formed African political parties, trade unions, and student associations were represented. It may seem ironic that Pan-Africanism thrived in the metropoles, but it was in cities like London and Paris where African workers, students, and intellectuals of diverse origin met, learned about one another's struggles, and forged a common African identity. In attendance at the Manchester congress were future African leaders like Nkrumah and Kenyatta, who as students abroad were exposed to the writings of Washington, Garvey, Du Bois, and others.

Historians have emphasized the ideological differences and personal rivalries between Du Bois and Garvey and, more specifically in American history, the conflicting ideas of Du Bois and Washington, but in fact Africans drew inspiration from all of them. Nkrumah's Ghana exemplifies these complimentary influences: Garvey's black star was placed in the center of the new nation's flag, and Du Bois, exiled from the United States because of his membership in the Communist party, spent the last few years of his life living in the Ghanaian capital of Accra, where he remains buried.

SECOND WORLD WAR IMPACT

One of the most influential events in the history of Pan-Africanism was the Italian invasion of Ethiopia in 1935. This was a hugely symbolic setback for Africans, so long after the Scramble for Africa, as one of the only two African countries that had been able to retain its independence, though completely surrounded by European colonial powers, was conquered and occupied. The army of Ethiopian emperor Haile Selassie, despite his limited efforts to modernize it, was defeated by an Italian force of five hundred thousand soldiers. The Italian occupation of Ethiopia caused an outcry among black intellectuals and activists worldwide, and Selassie emerged as a spokesperson for resistance to European colonial rule.

What historians term African nationalism gathered speed in the years following the Second World War. The hypocrisy of the Allied powers, who enlisted African help in fighting fascism in order to defend democracy in Europe, as well as the wartime experiences of African soldiers who were used by the European powers to crush anticolonial rebellions in such faraway places as French-occupied Vietnam, shaped a new generation of resistance to European colonial rule. In fact, African veterans often were in the vanguard of protest, not only influenced by the aforementioned but also personally disillusioned by the failure of the European colonial powers to keep their promises of pensions and other benefits in exchange for enlistment. Furthermore, Africans turned the imperialist rhetoric of economic and social development against their colonizers, at first agitating for improved conditions within the colonial system but then suddenly, inspired by anticolonial struggles around the world, heightening those demands to outright independence.

Increasingly cognizant of their own hypocrisy, particularly after the establishment in 1945 of the United Nations, an international body designed to prevent war and promote freedom; burdened by the costs of maintaining their colonies; and not least of all, recognizing the moral high ground claimed by the Soviet Union in its support of colonized peoples, the European imperial powers began to offer concessions. After 1946, for example, France extended political participation to more Africans in its colonies at three levels: within the colony, at the territorial stage, and in the metropole. After a series of boycotts, strikes, and protests as part of the Positive Action campaign called by the anticolonial Convention People's Party, the British invited Nkrumah to form a cabinet in the Gold Coast, essentially agreeing to an African-led colonial administration. While the pace of reforms and the march toward independence accelerated across the continent, it is important to remember the intransigence of colonial authorities and European settlers in such territories as Algeria, Kenya, and South Africa, where the anticolonial struggle was brutally suppressed.

Nevertheless, by 1960, known as the Year for Africa, most colonies in Africa were granted independence by the British and French. De Gaulle, the French president, first offered Africans a stark choice in 1958: complete independence or semiautonomy in a French-dominated union. Only one territory, Guinea, under the leadership of the radical trade unionist Sékou Touré, chose the former by referendum, and French retaliation was swift and cruel: before abruptly departing, French colonial officials destroyed the country's infrastructure, even smashing windows and furniture, and the French government severed all ties to its former colony. In an act of solidarity, Nkrumah, as leader of the only other independent sub-Saharan African country, offered financial assistance to Guinea, and the favor was later returned when Touré proclaimed Nkrumah co-president after the latter's overthrow in a military coup in 1966. Despite its vengeful behavior, France granted independence to its remaining African colonies (with the notable exception of Algeria) in the momentous year of 1960.

MARXISM

In the following decade, the influence of Marxism and the role of the Soviet Union and its allies became more prominent in Africa. One of the early flashpoints in the rivalry between the world's two superpowers occurred in the Congo, a huge country, so devastatingly exploited by the Belgians, where only a handful of African university graduates resided at independence in 1960. Congo's first leader, Patrice Lumumba, a former postal clerk who rose to prominence during the anticolonial struggle but who faced a series of crises immediately after assuming office, reportedly infuriated Belgian officials in attendance at the speech he delivered at the independence day celebrations on July 4. Describing the long struggle of the Congolese people against Belgian rule, he said:

> This was our fate for 80 years of a colonial regime; our wounds are too fresh and too painful still for us to drive them from our memory. We have known harassing work, exacted in exchange for salaries which did not permit us to eat enough to drive away hunger, or to clothe ourselves, or to house ourselves decently, or to raise our children as creatures dear to us.
>
> We have known ironies, insults, blows that we endured morning, noon and evening, because we are Negroes. Who will forget that to a Black one said "tu", certainly not as to a friend, but because the more honorable "vous" was reserved for whites alone?
>
> We have seen our lands seized in the name of allegedly legal laws, which in fact recognized only that might is right. We have seen that the law was not the same for a white and for a Black—accommodating for the first, cruel and inhuman for the other.
>
> We have witnessed atrocious sufferings of those condemned for their political opinions or religious beliefs, exiled in their own country, their fate truly worse than death itself.
>
> We have seen that in the towns there were magnificent houses for the whites and crumbling shanties for the Blacks; that a Black was not admitted in the motion-picture houses, in the restaurants, in the stores of the Europeans; that a Black traveled in the holds, at the feet of the whites in their luxury cabins.

> Who will ever forget the massacres where so many of our brothers perished,
> the cells into which those who refused to submit to a regime of oppression and
> exploitation were thrown?
> All that, my brothers, we have endured.

While Lumumba certainly was speaking the truth, his former colonial masters were offended by what they considered a break with diplomatic protocol. That was the least of Lumumba's worries, as in the week after independence he faced an army mutiny and the arrival of Belgian troops, allegedly to protect Europeans in the Congo. Soon thereafter, two of Congo's most mineral-rich provinces, Katanga and Kasai, declared secession. Lumumba's supporters in Congo and outside, including Nkrumah, claimed that Belgium and other Western powers, including the United States, were deliberately undermining him and planning a coup. They appealed to the United Nations, which sent peacekeepers, albeit it with a very limited mandate, in mid-July. His detractors accused Lumumba of being a communist, supported and directed by the Soviets, and incapable of ruling the Congo. By September, an army colonel named Joseph Mobutu had taken control of the city of Leopoldville, and in December his troops kidnapped Lumumba, who was found dead in February the following year. The Congo Crisis, as it became known, continued over the following few years until Mobuto seized power, remaining Congo's ruler until 1997. A brutal despot who enriched himself, neglected the development of his country, and allowed Western companies unfettered control of Congo's vast resources, Mobutu was backed throughout his reign by the United States.

Indeed, the alliances of the Cold War era in Africa may seem improbable to readers, but during this era U.S. foreign policy was driven by one exclusive goal, namely, the containment of communism in defense of capitalism. For the many Africans who remained under the rule of European imperial powers and minority regimes, however, communism, as an alternative system that promised self-determination and equality, held great appeal. While today we know that its system was characterized also by political repression, the Soviet Union not only represented hope for colonized Africans but, perhaps just as important, offered material aid and moral support to their anticolonial movements. Moreover, Africans drew inspiration from the revolutions in China in 1949 and Cuba a decade later, particularly since those countries also had experienced colonial rule and with only limited resources and mostly rural, illiterate populations were able to wage successful guerrilla struggles. Revolutionary China, under the leadership of Mao Tse-tung, provided aid to a number of anticolonial movements and progressive governments in Africa, most significantly Tanzania and Zambia, which were linked by the famous Chinese-built Tanzam railway. Even more remarkable, considering its small size and limited resources, in addition to an American blockade, Cuba under the leadership of Fidel Castro assumed a leading role in supporting liberation movements across Africa, a policy initiated during Che Guevara's Africa tour in 1964. During this visit to several African countries, the Cuban revolutionary hero made contact with leaders of guerrilla movements, particularly those in the Portuguese colonies, and offered Cuban military, technical, and medical assistance. Within months, Cuban military advisors and doctors were arriving in places like Portuguese Guinea, where they remained throughout the armed struggle and continued to work after independence was won in 1974. But the most significant contribution made by Cuba was to the liberation of southern Africa, the last region of the continent to win its independence from European rule.

SOUTH AFRICA

Throughout the decades described above, during which Africans across the continent regained their freedom, conditions for Africans in the southern tip of the continent worsened. The apartheid laws created by the Afrikaner National Party after its election to power in 1948—with such names as the Prohibition of Mixed Marriages Act (1949), the Population Registration Act (1950), the Group Areas Act (1950), and the Bantu Education Act (1953)—fully controlled African life, limiting who Africans could marry, determining where they could live, restricting their movements, and proscribing what they could learn. These laws also strictly segregated South Africa's diverse ethnic groups, with Europeans alone enjoying some degree of political and economic freedom at the expense of the African and Asian as well as the so-called Coloured populations. The oppressive conditions in South Africa were well known around the world, especially after the Sharpeville Massacre in March 1960, when sixty-nine protesters were shot dead by the police. The banning of the African National Congress (ANC) and the South African Communist Party (SACP), the two leading organizations protesting apartheid policies and both committed to a nonracial, democratic South Africa, forced its members to go underground, into exile, and to take up arms. As the situation further deteriorated, exemplified by the so-called forced removals, when African townships were destroyed, and the creation of the Bantustans, homelands for Africans in isolated and impoverished parts of the country, the number of South Africans who left the country increased. Some traveled to the Soviet Union, East Germany, and other communist countries, where they undertook academic studies and military training, while others resettled in neighboring African countries that also provided support to the antiapartheid movement. By the late 1970s, the South African apartheid regime was surrounded by what they perceived to be hostile, radical nations, such as Mozambique and Angola, both ruled by Marxist parties, and, in 1980, by African-ruled Zimbabwe, but retained the support of the United States and other European powers by successfully propagandizing itself as the last defense of capitalism and Christianity in Africa. The South African military regularly carried out bombing raids in neighboring countries and as far away as Lusaka, the capital of Zambia, where the ANC had its headquarters.

South Africa's most extensive military engagement, and the one in which its army was ultimately defeated, was in Angola, another flashpoint in the Cold War. After the Portuguese withdrew in 1974, the Soviet-backed People's Movement for the Liberation of Angola (MPLA), the most popular of three major guerrilla armies that fought against colonial rule, took power in the capital of Luanda. The MPLA's chief rival, the National Union for the Total Independence of Angola (UNITA), continued combat, backed by the United States and apartheid South Africa, both of which feared a Soviet presence in southern Africa. Over the next decade and a half, war raged in Angola as the MPLA and UNITA fought each other, South Africa invaded from its neighboring colony of South-West Africa, and Cuba, from across the ocean, sent tens of thousands of soldiers and massive amounts of military material, claiming it was defending the sovereignty of Angola. What historians have described as a superpower proxy battle between American-backed South Africa and Soviet-supported Cuba, ended in the famous battle in the Angolan city of Cuito Cuanavale in March 1988, when the combined forces consisting of fighters from the Cuban army, the MPLA, South Africa's ANC, and the South-West Africa People's Organization, defeated the South African apartheid army.

Following historic negotiations between South Africa and the United States on one side and the Soviet Union and Cuba on the other, a series of events marking the end of European rule in Africa took place. First, in February 1990, after twenty-seven years in prison, most of them spent on the infamous Robben Island, Nelson Mandela was released from prison. The following month, South-West Africa, renamed Namibia, gained its independence from South Africa. That same year, the ANC and SACP were legalized in South Africa, and Mandela, along with leaders of both parties, entered into negotiations with the apartheid regime that over the next few years led to the dismantling of apartheid, culminating in Mandela's election as president in 1994, the first vote in the history of South Africa in which Africans participated.

This is not to suggest that the end of apartheid and all the events leading to it in the early 1990s were solely the result of the victory at Cuito Cuanavale. Indeed, despite brutal repression by the police and other bodies of the apartheid state, South Africans continued to protest against apartheid, under auspices not only of the ANC and SACP but also of other prominent influential organizations, such as the Pan

A year after his release from prison, and in the midst of negotiations to end white minority rule in South Africa, future president Nelson Mandela, pictured here with Fidel Castro, visited Cuba in July 1991 to thank that nation for its support of the antiapartheid struggle. Mandela told the thousands of Cubans who had gathered in Matanzas: "Your crushing defeat of the racist army at Cuito Cuanavale was a victory for the whole of Africa!"

African Congress, inspired by the ideology of Black Consciousness articulated by the murdered antiapartheid activist Steve Biko, and the Christian churches, from which such key leaders as Desmond Tutu emerged. In addition, through the efforts of antiapartheid activists worldwide, including in the United States (where the administration of President Ronald Reagan, espousing a policy of "constructive engagement," provided critical support for the apartheid regime), a campaign for economic sanctions in which universities and corporations were pressured to divest successfully crippled the South African economy. Of course, even considering the primary role played by ordinary people in defeating the apartheid system, the perseverance, strength, and wisdom of South African leaders like Mandela cannot be underestimated.

Mandela himself, in a speech to tens of thousands in the Cuban city of Matanzas in July 1991, acknowledged the contributions of Cuba to the liberation of southern Africa and paid tribute to the inspiration that the Cuban revolution provided to colonized Africans.

We have long wanted to visit your country and express the many feelings that we have about the Cuban revolution, about the role of Cuba in Africa, southern Africa, and the world.

The Cuban people hold a special place in the hearts of the people of Africa. The Cuban internationalists have made a contribution to African independence, freedom, and justice, unparalleled for its principled and selfless character.

From its earliest days the Cuban revolution has itself been a source of inspiration to all freedom-loving people. ...

Your crushing defeat of the racist army at Cuito Cuanavale was a victory for the whole of Africa!

The overwhelming defeat of the racist army at Cuito Cuanavale provided the possibility for Angola to enjoy peace and consolidate its own sovereignty!

The defeat of the racist army allowed the struggling people of South Africa to finally win their independence!

The decisive defeat of the apartheid aggressors broke the myth of the invincibility of the white oppressors!

The defeat of the apartheid army was an inspiration to the struggling people inside South Africa!

Without the defeat of Cuito Cuanavale our organization would not have been unbanned!

The defeat of the racist army at Cuito Cuanavale has made it possible for me to be here today!

Cuito Cuanavale was a milestone in the history of the struggle for southern African liberation!

For many Africans it was fitting, in the spirit of Pan-Africanism and Marxism, that the army defending the last bastion of European rule on the continent, nearly three decades after the Year of Africa and more than four centuries after the first European settlers arrived in South Africa, was defeated by forces comprising diasporic Africans from a socialist country. In many ways, the end of European colonial rule came full circle, with the influences on Africa's anticolonial movements all represented at that epic battle at Cuito Cuanavale.

CONCLUSION

Almost two decades have passed since South Africa's independence from European rule, and during that time the world has experienced dramatic changes, principally the collapse of the Soviet Union. Nevertheless, Cuba remains a country committed to socialism and providing assistance to African countries, China has emerged as a new power on the African continent, and the dream of Pan-Africanism, despite many setbacks during the postcolonial era, remains alive and well, as evidenced by the formation of the African Union in 2001. The struggle for independence across Africa took on many forms and faced different obstacles but everywhere was ultimately successful. In their fight against European colonial rule, Africans were inspired by a range of ideologies rooted in identity, politics, and religion. Often these were complementary, though sometimes in opposition, and must be understood in the larger context of recent world history, not only in terms of the Cold War but also in relation to the struggles of colonized and newly independent peoples outside of Africa. As part of what has been variously termed the Third World, the developing world, and the Global South, Africans share the experience of European colonial rule and the challenges of postcolonial economic and political realities with the majority population of the world. Like them, Africans continue to reflect on the colonial era and its significance on the present.

REFERENCES

Cooper, Frederick. *Africa since 1940: The Past of the Present* (Cambridge: Cambridge University Press, 2002).

Nugent, Paul. *Africa since Independence: A Comparative History* (New York: Palgrave Macmillan, 2004).

Pan-Africanism
Davidson, Basil. Black Star: *A View of the Life and Times of Kwame Nkrumah* (Oxford: James Currey, 2007).

Marxism
De Witte, Ludo. *The Assassination of Lumumba* (London: Verso, 2001).

Gleijeses, Piero. *Conflicting Missions: Havana, Washington, and Africa, 1959–1976* (Chapel Hill, University of North Carolina Press, 2002).

South Africa
Mandela, Nelson, and Fidel Castro. *How Far We Slaves Have Come!* (New York: Pathfinder, 1991).

Conclusion

For most of Africa, over half a century has passed since the end of European colonial rule. What this means, of course, is that the majority of Africans have no direct experience of colonialism and that for those who do, it is a distant memory in spite of the richness and diversity of oral histories from across the continent. This book began by presenting scholarly arguments about the significance of the colonial period to African history. And while we may dispute over emphasizing its importance in the long history of Africa, the preceding chapters clearly show that colonialism impacted Africa in myriad economic, political, social, and cultural ways. These legacies are evident across Africa today, yet Africans continue to debate how much the colonial experience has shaped the present. Is the colonial period so far in the past, followed by so many decades of global change and events, including the collapse of the Soviet Union and then the end of the Cold War, that it is disingenuous to blame it for the problems of contemporary Africa? Or was colonialism so transformative, laying the foundations for neocolonial economic and political relations between Africa and the West, that it is right to trace Africa's troubles back to European conquest?

This debate is not simply rhetorical; it is relevant to the lives of ordinary Africans today. It is playing out right now in a case brought by four Mau Mau veterans against the British government. The Kenyans are suing the Foreign Office claiming they were tortured

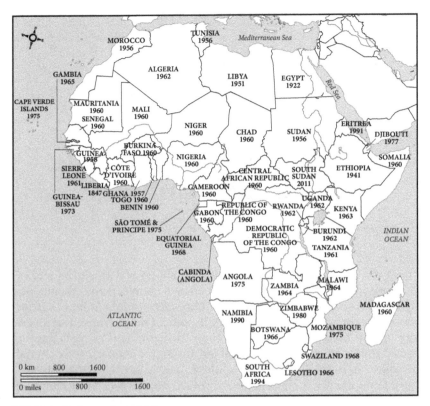

MOROCCO 1956

TUNISIA 1956

Mediterranean Sea

GAMBIA 1965

ALGERIA 1962

LIBYA 1951

EGYPT 1922

Red Sea

CAPE VERDE ISLANDS 1975

MAURITANIA 1960

MALI 1960

SENEGAL 1960

NIGER 1960

CHAD 1960

SUDAN 1956

ERITREA 1991

DJIBOUTI 1977

BURKINA FASO 1960

GUINEA 1958

NIGERIA 1960

SOMALIA 1960

SIERRA LEONE 1961

CÔTE D'IVOIRE 1960

LIBERIA 1847

GHANA 1957

TOGO 1960

CAMEROON 1960

CENTRAL AFRICAN REPUBLIC 1960

SOUTH SUDAN 2011

ETHIOPIA 1941

GUINEA-BISSAU 1973

BENIN 1960

SÃO TOMÉ & PRINCIPE 1975

REPUBLIC OF THE CONGO 1960

GABON 1960

RWANDA 1962

UGANDA 1962

KENYA 1963

EQUATORIAL GUINEA 1968

DEMOCRATIC REPUBLIC OF THE CONGO 1960

BURUNDI 1962

TANZANIA 1961

INDIAN OCEAN

CABINDA (ANGOLA) 1975

ANGOLA 1975

ZAMBIA 1964

MALAWI 1964

MADAGASCAR 1960

ATLANTIC OCEAN

NAMIBIA 1990

ZIMBABWE 1980

BOTSWANA 1966

MOZAMBIQUE 1975

SWAZILAND 1968

SOUTH AFRICA 1994

LESOTHO 1966

0 km   800   1600

0 miles   800   1600

MAP 5   Independent Africa

by the British during the insurgency in the 1950s and 1960s. Two men allege they were castrated, another man says he was beaten unconscious during an incident that resulted in the deaths of eleven other men, and a woman claims she was raped. For this group of elderly Kenyans, the abuses they suffered undoubtedly and profoundly affected their lives over the past half century. Their memories of colonialism are vivid and painful, and they are seeking an official apology as well as the establishment of a trust fund to support fellow Mau Mau veterans. The British government at first tried to argue, without irony, that the case should be brought against the government of Kenya since it had assumed all responsibilities for the war at independence. When this strategy failed, as the British High Court gave permission for the veterans to sue the British government, officials suggested that the case was baseless as too many years have passed since the alleged incidents and too many witnesses have died. Meanwhile, in 2011 scholars and activists discovered thousands of documents, assumed lost, in the Foreign Office's archives, some of which detail abuses by British colonial officials in the Mau Mau detention camps.

Beyond personal experiences, memories, and suffering, colonialism certainly impacted Africa in larger, broader, structural ways. Only a few years after the independence of Ghana, Nkrumah wrote the book *Neo-Colonialism: The Last Stage of Imperialism*, an update to the treatise by Lenin discussed at the start of chapter 1. In it Nkrumah argues that despite political independence, African countries remain economically dependent on their former colonial rulers and other Western countries like the United States not by choice, but because of the realities of the global capitalist economy. One important example is that the prices of cash crops are not determined by African producers but by market speculators in the West. In short, African countries may have their own flags, stamps, and embassies, but they do not have control over their own economic affairs. Nkrumah thus maintains that political independence is worthless unless a nation possesses economic sovereignty as well.

Indeed, the thrill and hope of the 1960s subsided as the many problems new African countries faced became evident. The Kenyan environmentalist and Nobel Prize winner Wangari Maathai captures the mood of that time in her final book, *The Challenge for Africa*. The following extended excerpt catalogs the harsh realities of independence:

It is perhaps hard, looking back, to capture the excitement of the early years of independence, and how rapidly the transition took place. In January 1966, when I was twenty-five, I returned to Kenya, having completed my undergraduate and master's degree in the United States. Six years earlier, I had gone to the United States as part of the Kennedy "lift," a visionary attempt to educate a generation of East African leaders to meet the challenges of independence. The initiative was supported by the U.S. Department of State and members of the prominent political family the Kennedys.

When I left Kenya, Jomo Kenyatta, the president of the Kenya African National Union (KANU), then a leading pro-independence party, was still in internal exile, and the country was under a state of emergency imposed in 1952 by the British colonial administration after the outbreak of the Mau Mau war of liberation. When I returned, Kenya was independent, and Kenyatta was the first president. During the years I was away, Nigeria, Mauritania, Sierra Leone, Tanzania, Rwanda, Burundi, Algeria, Uganda, Malawi, Zambia, the Gambia, Botswana, and Lesotho also achieved independence. I remember the exultation that I and many other young Africans felt then and the commitment we shared to build the newly emerging countries that were now fully ours, on a continent returning to African control.

Disappointment lay ahead. By and large, newly independent nations made no efforts to change the inherited colonial systems of governance, even though they had been designed, principally, to facilitate the continued exploitation of human and natural resources of the colonies for the benefit of the colonial motherland. And, although they were relinquishing direct rule over their colonies, the European powers were eager to maintain economic ties with the new states and ensure a steady supply of the raw natural resources that had provided their countries with such wealth during the colonial period. The departing administrators made sure that the leaders who eventually held power in the former colonies were as cooperative politically as they were pliant economically. For all practical purposes, it was simply a change of guards. Those leaders, like Julius Nyerere of Tanzania, who sought to remain nonaligned and who tried to forge a different path of development were isolated, vilified, and denied support.

At the same time, those leaders who toed the line were rewarded with political protection from would-be plotters of coup d'états. They were given economic assistance they did not have to account for, such as opportunities to open secret bank accounts or purchase expensive villas in foreign capitals. Their armies were well supplied with weapons and equipment, which were used mostly to silence their own citizens. These regimes violated human rights and remained unquestioned by those colonies powers that considered themselves defenders of freedom and democracy.

Such was the legacy of colonialism in the newly independent states of Africa: it left the African people chained to a new form of oppression. (29–30)

Maathai's words are reflective of a prevailing sentiment among most Africans, one that attributes many of the ills of Africa to the economic and political legacies of European colonial rule yet at the same time recognizes the failings of Africa's leaders, largely the products and defenders of that colonial legacy. In fact, in many ways, Africa's postcolonial rulers, with major exceptions, such as the aforementioned Nyerere and Nkrumah, have been dismissed as puppets of their former colonial masters. And, more radically, some Africans extend the critique to all members of what is termed the African elite, professionals and entrepreneurs at the economic top of society, who, it is held, benefit most from the neocolonial arrangement.

In popular culture, these elites often are characterized as Africans mimicking Europeans. This critique is best exemplified by the lyrics of the world-renowned Nigerian musician Fela Kuti, whose mother was a prominent figure in the anticolonial movement. Fela, as he was known, often mocked Africans who he believed blindly followed European customs. His song "Gentleman," for instance, pokes fun of African men who wear Western-style suits in the tropical climate of Africa. Typical of much of his music, the lyrics are written in what is commonly known as Nigerian Pidgin English and include profanity:

> No be gentle man at all oh
> I be African man original
> I no be gentle man at all oh
> I be African man original
> I no be gentle man at all oh
> Africa hot I like am so
> I no want to wear
> But my friend don't know
> He put him socks
> He put him shoe
> He put him pant
> He put him singlet
> He put him trouser
> He put him shirt
> He put him tie
> He put him coat
> He come cover all with him hat
> He be gentle man
> He go sweat
> All over
> He go faint
> Lie down
> He go smell
> like shit
> He go piss for body
> E no go know
> I no be gentle man like that

Fela's biting depiction of an African "gentleman" is sarcastic, of course, but symbolic of the larger notion that so-called Westernized Africans are out of touch with their roots and too eager to adopt a foreign culture while denying their own. Many have argued that Fela took his insistence on authenticity too far and practiced it erroneously, as when he appeared in public wearing only a small covering over his genitals. Yet like many artists who criticize social mores and society's elite, his rhetoric and behavior were exaggerated to express widely held opinions.

Despite these critical perspectives on the economic, political, and cultural effects of European colonial rule in Africa, many of the social and cultural institutions that today flourish through the enthusiastic initiative of Africans themselves can be traced back to that era. In a series of lectures about colonialism and its legacy in Africa, historian A. Adu Boahen presented a list of what he considered to be positive impacts of European colonial rule in Africa, including peace and stability after the early colonial period; the establishment of Africa's future nations with clearly defined boundaries; the emergence of national and Pan-African identities among Africans; the construction of each country's basic infrastructure during the colonial era and development of primary commodity production; population growth, social mobility, and urbanization; and, finally, the spread of Christianity, Islam, and Western education. Certainly anyone who read the preceding chapters will find fault with this list of positive impacts. And Boahen himself qualifies each of these with the negative consequences as well. For example, he points out the arbitrary nature of Africa's boundaries, the resultant border disputes between African nations, and the dysfunctional nature of some of these states because of their sheer size or lack of natural resources. Yet Boahen's position is that there are both positive and negative legacies of European colonial rule in Africa, plus and minus sides of a "balance sheet" that, as he puts it, typifies many Africans' assessment of the colonial legacy. This is in sharp contrast to the conclusions of such radical scholars as Walter Rodney, who famously wrote, "Colonialism had only one hand—it was a one-armed bandit."

Nevertheless, it is safe to assume that most Africans would agree with Boahen's conclusion that "though colonialism was a mere episode lasting no more than a hundred years anywhere in Africa, it was nonetheless an extremely important one. It marks a clear watershed in the history of the continent, and Africa's subsequent development is bound to be very much determined by some of its legacies" (111).

REFERENCES

Maathai, Wangari. *The Challenge for Africa* (New York: Pantheon Books, 2009).

Nkrumah, Kwame. *Neo-Colonialism: The Highest Stage of Imperialism* (New York: International Publishers, 1965).

Index

INDEX